Easy to Crochet
Potholders

First published in the United States of America in 2010 by
Trafalgar Square Books
North Pomfret, Vermont 05053

Printed in China

Originally published in Germany as **Klassische Topflappen**

Copyright © 2009 frechverlag GmbH, Stuttgart, Germany (www.frechverlag.de)
English translation © 2010 Trafalgar Square Books

This edition is published by arrangement with Claudia Böhme Rights & Literary Agency, Hannover, Germany
(www.agency-boehme.com)

ISBN: 978-1-57076-450-9

Library of Congress Control Number: 2010920046

Translation from German: C. Elizabeth Wellenstein
We wish to thank the companies Coats, Coats LLC, Kenzingen, www.coatsgmbh.de for the support of this book.
Project Management: Hannelore Irmer-Romeo
Editor: Cosima Kroll
Layout: Petra Theilfarth
Photos: Frechverlag LLC 70499 Stuttgart; lighting Michael Ruder, Stuttgart

10 9 8 7 6 5 4 3 2 1

Table of Contents

Preface

Potholders are simply indispensable and found in every kitchen. Practical, as well as pretty, in rosette and blossom shapes, in different textures, or in amusing themes. Every kitchen needs a classic potholder with stripes, a Spotted Cow, a Heart with little Roses or a Cheerful Duckling in an Egg to hang on the wall.

The patterns shown can be made to match kitchen furnishings as well as your personal tastes, with little expense. With over 25 inspiring, fun-to-crochet patterns in this book, let your imagination run wild as you play with colors and designs.

Crocheting a potholder is a great way to use up remnants from your yarn stash. Whether it's to brighten up your own kitchen or make as a gift, there are patterns for all tastes and seasons.

I hope you'll enjoy many fun-filled, relaxing hours with your crocheting.

GLOSSARY OF TERMS

CLASSIC POTHOLDERS IN TRADITIONAL COLORS! Here is where you'll find the information you need to begin right away. If you are new to crochet, please take a look at the basics first. You'll find detailed illustrations and descriptions about how to:

• begin a ring

• how to work with more than one color

• increase and decrease in both single and multiple colors

• how to treble and double treble crochet

• how to finish a ring with a slip stitch or a "mouse-tooth" picot edge

The embroidery which embellishes many of the potholders has been clearly illustrated and explained.

You'll find the instructions and stitch diagrams for each pattern either before or after each photograph.

Adjustable Ring

Place the working strand (the ball yarn) over the loose end (cross over) then pull the tail end through the loop. This way the size of the yarn ring is can be adjusted to the desired size after the potholder is completed.

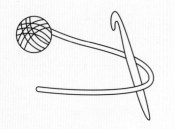

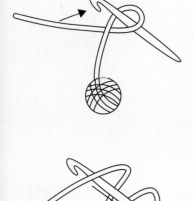

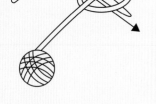

Decrease Stitches

Decrease One Stitch

At the beginning of the row, draw yarn through the first and second stitches together. At the end of the row, draw yarn through the last two stitches together.

Decrease More Than One Stitch

At the beginning of the row, slip stitch the number of stitches to be decreased. At the end of the row, leave the number of stitches to be decreased un-worked.

Let's say, for example you want to decrease 4 stitches at the beginning of a row. Slip stitch over first 3 stitches then join following 2 stitches together. If you'd like to decrease 4 stitches at the end of a row, join the 5th and 4th stitches from the end together and leave the following 3 stitches from the end unworked.

Increase Stitches

Increase one stitch

At the beginning of a row, work 2 sc into the 1st stitch of the previous row. At the end of the row, work 2 sc into the last stitch of the previous row.

Increase More Than One Stitch at the Beginning of a Row (not pictured)

At the end of the previous row, ch 1 for every stitch you want to add, and ch 1 to turn. After the turn, work sc into 2nd ch from the hook.

Increase More Than One Stitch at the End of a Row

Work each st at the end of the row into the loop of the row below. For the 1st increase, go into the center of the previous st, pull through 1 loop, 1 yo, pull through both sts. For every additional increase, go into the center of the loop of the row below, pull loop through, 1 yo, pull through both sts.

Crochet In The Round

The round potholders are worked in a spiral. Running a colored thread between stitches at the end of a round makes counting easier. For increasing as stated in the instructions, double the number of stitches by working 2 sc into one stitch.

Changing Colors

When changing colors, hold strand of unused thread along the top of the previous row of sc and catch at each stitch of the new row. When working with large areas of color change, work with several balls of yarn. When changing colors, work the last stitch of the old color along with the first stitch of the new color.

Abbreviations

ch = chain stitch

dc = double crochet

dec = decrease

hdc = half double crochet

inc = increase

ndl(s) = needle(s)

rem = remaining

rep = repeat

rnd(s) = round(s)

sc = single crochet

sl st = slip stitch

st(s) = stitch(es)

tog = together

tr = treble crochet

yo = yarnover

Crocheting With More Than One Color

When working a pattern with several colors, catch one of the unused strands on every stitch. Alternate which unused color is caught on every 2nd or 3rd stitch. That way the potholder won't be too bulky and the stranding won't show on the front of the potholder.

Treble Crochet

Bring yarn twice over the hook (from back to front), skip the first four chains, then insert hook into the fifth chain from the hook (or indicated stitch). Yo and draw through chain stitch. Yo and draw it through the first two loops on the hook. Yo again and draw it through the next two loops on the hook. Yo and draw it through both remaining loops on the hook.

Double Treble Crochet

Bring yarn over hook 3 times, insert hook into the 6th st (or indicated stitch), yo, draw loop through, [yo, draw through 2 lps on hook] 4 times.

"Mouse-Tooth" Picot

*Ch 3 and then slip stitch into 1st ch (or indicated stitch), skip 1 stitch of previous rnd, sc into next stitch; rep from * around.

"Crab" Stitch

This is a simple single crochet stitch which, in contrast to all other crochet techniques, is worked from left to right. If worked from the right side, the crab sts lay like little cords around the edge. If worked from the wrong side, you'll create a dainty edge, which resembles cross stitch. If you'd like a wider edge, crochet another one or more rows of single crochet and then work the crab stitches.

The patterns are classified by level of difficulty as follows:

 1 = beginner

 2 = intermediate

 3 = experienced

Embroidery Stitches

Several different embroidery stitches are used to embellish some of the patterns. The specific stitch used will be noted in the pattern instructions. The pictures here show the step-by-step instructions for each individual stitch. In the pictures, the stitch has been enlarged.

Cross Stitch

Cross stitch consists of a foundation stitch and a cover stitch. The foundation stitch is worked from the lower left to the upper right. The cover stitch is worked from the lower right to the upper left. The stitches are made in rows. Start by leaving a tail of floss about 2 in long. It will get sewn in just as the end of the floss will, before a new strand is started.

In the pictures, the stitches have been enlarged and are shown here on a 4 x 4 grid, making the embroidery easy to see.

Foundation Stitch

The embroidery begins at the upper left. Start by pulling the strand through the fabric from back to front. Count 4 strands to the right, then 4 strands up and insert needle from front to back. Bring needle out again 4 strands directly below. Repeat foundation stitch, according to pattern, until color changes.

Cover Stitch

The return row begins with the cover stitch. Count 4 strands to the left and then 4 strands up and insert needle. Work as many cover stitches as there are foundation stitches. This is how to make a nice straight row of little crosses on the right side of your work. On the wrong side you'll see a series of vertical stitches.

Daisy Stitch

Chain Stitch

Secure your thread to the back of your work. Bring the needle through to the right side on the line you want to follow. Go back down as close as possible to your starting point and bring the needle back up a short distance along the line of the pattern. Before you pull the needle through the fabric, make sure that the working thread is underneath the needle. Then pull the needle through forming a loop or chain on the surface. Re-insert the needle, next to where it came through the fabric, inside the loop of the first chain stitch and again, bring it up further along the line. Tuck the thread under the needle and pull it through to make the second chain stitch.

Stem Stitch

Work from left to right, taking regular small stitches along the line of the design. Bring needle up through fabric, holding the thread toward you as shown. Make a short slanting back stitch along line. Make the next and each successive stitch from right to left and bring the needle out to the left at the end of previous stitch.

TEXTURED
POTHOLDERS

IN THE CLASSIC COLORS OF RED, BLUE, WHITE, GREEN AND YELLOW! Textured potholders are simply charming in these enduring colors and patterns. Whether in waffle patterns, checkered patterns or zig-zags, these potholders are classics. Crocheted in bright colors and simple designs, they are eye-catching as well as useful in the kitchen.

Checkered Pattern

Level of Difficulty
Beginner

Measurements
Approx 8 ¼ x 8 ¾ in
(21 x 22 cm)

Materials
Schachenmayr Catania
in White (color 106)
and Peacock (color
146), 100g each and
Red (color 115), 50g

Hook: US size C
(2.5 mm)

Gauge
18 sts and 20 rows =
4 x 4 in (10 x 10 cm)

Pattern Stitch
Sc worked back and forth. Turn every row with ch 1.

Instructions
Ch 50 to turn with white. Work according to pattern. When changing colors, begin the sc with the old color (bring working yarn through loops of st below) and finish with new color through the two loops on hook. Hold strand of unused thread along the top of the previous row of sc and catch at each stitch of the new row.

Finishing
Finish the potholder by working sc in white all around. Work a closing rnd in peacock by working every 2nd sc of the previous rnd with 1 sc. Between each sc, work ch 2. For the hanging loop, ch 12 in peacock and cover chain with sc.

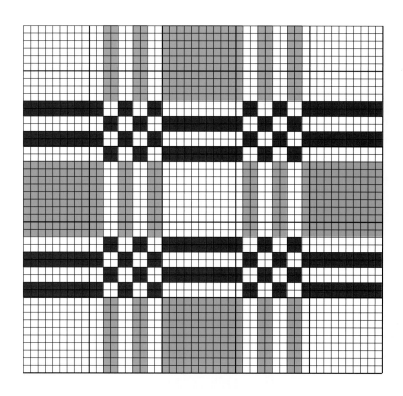

■ = 1 sc in peacock
■ = 1 sc in red
☐ = 1 sc in white

Red-White Zig-Zag

Level of Difficulty
Beginner

Measurements
Approx 8 ¼ x 8 ¾ in
(21 x 22 cm)

Materials
Schachenmayr Catania
in Red (color 115) and
White (color 106), 100g
each

Hook: US size C (2.5
mm)

Gauge
18 sts and 20 rows =
4 x 4 in (10 x 10 cm)

Pattern Stitch
Sc worked back and forth. Turn every row with ch 1.

Instructions
Ch 42 to turn with white.

Rows 1-3: With white, sc.

Row 4: With red, *1 sc, 1 sc (not in the sc of the previous (3rd row), but the sc of the row before that (2nd row), 1 sc (worked into the sc of the 1st white row), 1 sc into the 2nd row, rep from *, end with 1 sc.

Rows 5-7: With red, sc.

Row 8: With white, 1 sc, 1 sc (not in the sc of the previous row, but the sc of the 6th row), 1 sc (worked into the sc of the 5th row), 1 sc into the 6th row, rep from *, end with 1 sc.

Row 9-11: With white sc.

Rows 12-43: Repeat rows 4-11.

Rows 44-47: With red, repeat rows 4-7.

Row 48: With white, repeat the 8th row.

Row 49: With white, sc.

Finishing
Weave in the ends and with red, work a round of sc. Finally, with red work a double round of chain border (see Sweet Fruits, diagram C, p 23). For the hanging loop, ch 15 in red and cover in 1 rd sc.

Dutch Boys

Level of Difficulty
Beginner

Measurements
Approx 9 ½ x 10 ½ in
(23 x 26 cm)

Materials
Schachenmayr Catania
in Denim (color 164)
and White (color 106),
100g each

Hook: US size C
(2.5 mm)

Gauge
18 sts and 20 rows =
4 x 4 in (10 x 10 cm)

Pattern Stitch
Sc worked back and forth. Turn every row with ch 1.

Instructions
Ch 48 to turn. Follow chart. When changing colors, begin the sc with the old color (bring working yarn through loops of st below) and finish with new color through the two loops on hook. Hold strand of unused thread along the top of the previous row of sc and catch at each stitch of the new row.

Finishing
With denim, work once around in sc and then once around in "mouse-tooth" stitch. For the hanging loop, ch 12 in denim and cover in sc.

■ = 1 sc in denim
□ = 1 sc in white

Red and White Design

Level of Difficulty
Beginner

Measurements
Approx 8 x 8 in
(20 x 20 cm)

Materials
Schachenmayr Catania
in Red (color 115) and
White (color 106), 100g
each and Royal (color
201), small amount

Hook: US size C
(2.5 mm)

Gauge
18 sts and 20 rows =
4 x 4 in (10 x 10 cm)

Pattern Stitch
Sc worked back and forth. Turn every row with ch 1.

Instructions
When changing colors, begin the sc with the old color (bring working yarn through loops of st below) and finish with new color through the two loops on hook. Hold strand of unused thread along the top of the previous row of sc and catch at each stitch of the new row.

Row 1: Ch 49 to turn.
Row 2: Alternate 2 sc in red and 2 sc in white, end with 2 sc in white.
Row 3: 1 sc in white, alternate 2 sc in red and 2 sc in white, end with 1 sc in white.
Row 4: 2 sc in white, alternate 2 sc in red and 2 sc in white, end with 2 sc in red.
Row 5: 1 sc in red, alternate 2 sc in white and 2 sc in red, end with 1 sc in red.
Row 6: 2 sc in red, alternate 2 sc in white and 2 sc in red, end with 2 sc in white.
Row 7: 1 sc in white, alternate 2 sc in red and 2 sc in white, end with 1 sc in white.
Row 8: 2 sc in white, alternate 2 sc in royal and 2 sc in white, end with 2 sc in royal.
Row 9: 1 sc in royal, alternate 2 sc in white and 2 sc in royal, end with 1 sc in royal.
Row 10-33: Repeat rows 2-5.
Row 34: 2 sc in red, alternate 2 sc in white and 2 sc in red, end with 2 sc in white.
Row 35: 1 sc in white, alternate 2 sc in red and 2 sc in white, end with 1 sc in white.
Row 36: 2 sc in white, alternate 2 sc in royal and 2 sc in white, end with 2 sc in royal.
Row 37: 1 sc in royal, alternate 2 sc in white and 2 sc in royal, end with 1 sc in royal.
Row 38-41: Repeat rows 2-5.
Row 42: 2 sc in red, alternate 2 sc in white and 2 sc in red, end with 2 sc in white.
Row 43: 1 sc in white, alternate 2 sc in red and 2 sc in white, end with 1 sc in white.

Finishing
With white, sc once around. For the final rnd, with red, work 1 sc into every 2nd sc of the previous rnd. For the hanging loop, ch 12 in red and cover with sc.

Colorful Bands

Level of Difficulty
Beginner

Measurements
Approx. 8 1/4 x 8 1/4 in
(20 x 20 cm)

Materials
Shachenmayr Catania in
White (color 106), 100g,
Yellow (color 208),
Spring Green (color
170), Orange (color
189), Azure (color 174),
Red (color 115), Peacock
(color 146), Rose (color
158), Marine (color
124), Pistachio (color
236), Chestnut (color
157), Melon (color 235)
and Royal (color 201),
small amounts

Hook: US size C
(2.5 mm)

Gauge
18 sts and 20 rows =
4 x 4 in (10 x 10 cm)

Pattern Stitch
Double crochet worked
back and forth. Turn
every row with ch 1.

Potholder
Work Rows 1-20 with white as follows:
Row 1: Ch 48 to turn.
Row 2: Sc in 2nd ch from hook and in each ch across = 47 sc.
Row 3: 2 dc, *ch1, 1 dc, ch 1, 1 dc, (always skip 1 sc in previous row when working dc); rep from *and end with 2 dc (see chart below).
Rows 4-19: Work as for row 3.
Row 20: Sc across.

Bands
Make 17 bands in assorted colors. For each band, ch 50; turn and work 1 dc in each ch, starting in 2nd ch from hook = 49 dc.

Finishing
Weave the bands through the potholder mesh, working alternately over and under the double crochet posts and staggering the weaving from row to row. Finish the potholder by working sc in white all around, securing the bands at the edges as you work. Be careful not to work more than 2 sc in each band, otherwise the potholder will ripple. Next work a "mouse-tooth" edging around. For the hanging loop, with white, ch 12 and cover chain with sc.

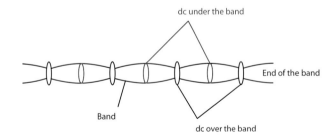

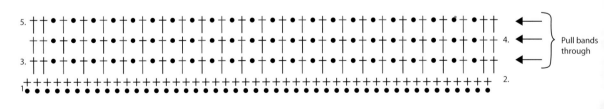

† = dc under the band   † = dc over the band   + = sc   ● = ch

Sweet Little Fruits

Level of Difficulty
Intermediate

Measurements
Approx 8 x 8 in
(20 x 20 cm)

Materials
Schachenmayr Catania
in White (color 106)
and Azure (color 174),
100g each, Yellow
(color 208), Red (color
115), Spring Green
(color 170) and Denim
(color 164), small
amounts

Hook: US size C
(2.5 mm)

Blunt-tipped tapestry
needle

Gauge
18 sts and 20 rows =
4 x 4 in (10 x 10 cm)

Chart
p 22

Diagrams A-C
p 23

Pattern Stitch
Sc worked back and forth. Turn every row with ch 1.

Instructions
Ch 46 to turn: ch 15 with white, ch 15 with azure, ch 15 with white. Continue, following chart on page 22, always twisting strands at the color change on WS. Finish by weaving in all tails on WS and then, with azure, work 1 rnd in sc around potholder. Finish with a double round of chain border (see Diagram C, p. 23). For the first rnd, sc with red into every 4th st of the azure row and follow each sc with ch 5 (at each corner of the potholder, work 1 sc in every 3rd st). Using white for the 2nd rnd, work 1 sc in the center of the 3 skipped sts of the azure rnd by working behind the red chain loop. When removing the hook from the sc of the previous rnd, go under the red chain loop and pull thread to front, ch 1, thus joining the red chain loop to the white. Next, ch 4 and continue around the red chain loops with 1 sc in the center of the next 3 skipped sts of the azure rnd; work as set around.

Finishing
Make hanging loop with red: ch 12 and cover with sc. Embroider the cherry and apple stems, lemon branch, and grape cluster tendrils with stem stitch (see Diagram B, p. 23). Outline the individual grapes in the cluster with a single strand of white yarn. Crochet the cherry, apple, and lemon leaves following chart on page 22. Crochet strawberry leaves following Chart A on p. 23 and sew fruit pieces onto potholder.

= 1 sc in Azure

= 1 sc in Red

= 1 sc in Yellow

= 1 sc in Denim

= 1 sc in Spring Green

= 1 sc in White

Leaf for cherries and lemon

Leaf for apple

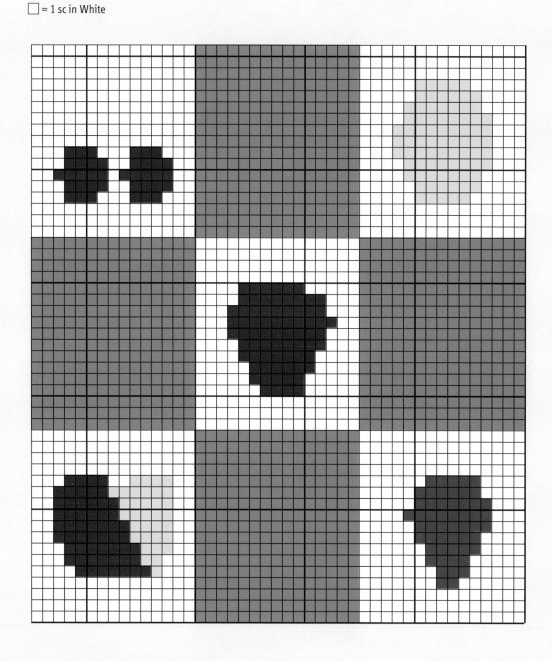

Diagram A

Leaf for Strawberry

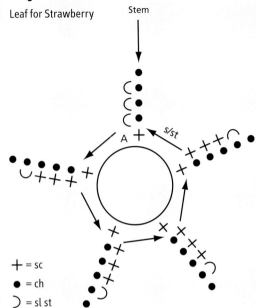

Stem

s/st

A

+ = sc

● = ch

⊃ = sl st

Diagram B

Pattern/Drawing of the Grape Tendrils

Diagram C

Work from front

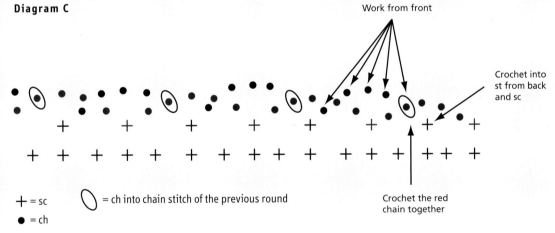

Crochet into
st from back
and sc

+ = sc   ⬭ = ch into chain stitch of the previous round

● = ch

Crochet the red
chain together

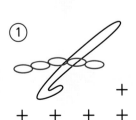

①

From the back,
sc 1 then pull needle
out of loop

②

From the front,
pick up loop and
ch 5. At the 1st ch,
crochet together
with the red chain.

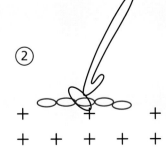

+ = sc

⬭ = ch

| 23

Waffle Pattern

Level of Difficulty
Beginner

Measurements
Approx 7 x 7 in
(18 x 18 cm)

Materials
Schachenmayr Catania
in Red (color 115), and
White (color 106), 50g
each and Royal (color
201) small amount

Hook: US size C
(2.5 mm)

Gauge
18 sts and 20 rows =
4 x 4 in (10 x 10 cm)

Diagrams A-C
p 26

Pattern Stitch

Dc in the rnd and in rows. Begin each rnd with a ch 1 and end each rnd with a sl st. Turn each row with a ch 1. The waffle pattern is a combination of regular double crochet and front post double crochet.

Instructions

Rnd 1: With red, ch 16 and close the ring with 1 sl st.
Rnd 2: Sc 26 around ch ring.

Begin working in rows from here on!

Row 1: In 8 sts of the previous rnd, work 8 dc, then ch 2 (you are building the corners of the potholder), then work another 8 dc into the next 8 sts of the previous rnd. The remaining 10 sc of the previous rnd are on hold for what will later become the hanging loop.
Row 2: From here on, work the dc waffle pattern. (see diagram B) Work the first and last pair of dc sts as regular dc. From the 3rd dc, alternate 2 front post and 2 regular dc. In the next row, repeat as above, shifting the dc. For the front post dc, yarn around hook, insert hook around post of dc in row below. Hook is inserted from right to left behind st (hook begins at front of work, between 2 dc, goes behind next st and out again to the front). With hook at front, on left side of dc post, bring yarn through and complete as for dc (yarn around hook and through 2 loops) 2 times. In the tip of the potholder (around the 2 ch sts of the previous row) work 2 dc, ch 2, 2 dc. Be aware that the 4 dc are worked around the ch 2 (the ch sts are worked around rather than into the sc sts).
Rows 3-21: Repeat row 2.

Color Pattern

Rnds 1- 2 and Rows 1-7: Work in red.
Rows 8-11, 12, 13: Work in white.
Rows 12-13: Work in royal.
Rows 14-17: Work in white.
Rows 18-21: Work in red.

Finishing

Work a double rnd of chain border in red and white as for Sweet Little Fruits, Diagram C, p 23. With white, cover the hanging loop in sc.

Diagram A

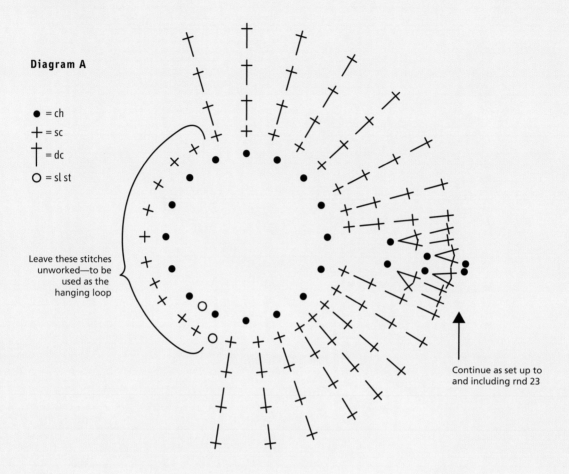

● = ch

✝ = sc

† = dc

O = sl st

Leave these stitches
unworked—to be
used as the
hanging loop

Continue as set up to
and including rnd 23

Diagram B
Waffle Pattern

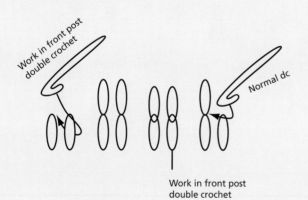

Work in front post
double crochet

Normal dc

Work in front post
double crochet

Diagram C

In every round, stagger/alternate the stitches
worked in front post double crochet

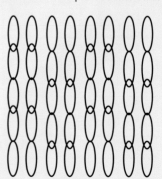

POTHOLDERS
WITH A THEME

DESIGNS FOR EVERY SEASON! The Easter Bunny, Santa Claus, and the Good Kitchen Ghost are all as enchanting as the magical slipper of 1001 Nights, the Duckling in an Egg, and the Little Dress Potholder.

Suitable for every occasion, décor and taste, you'll have no problem finding a potholder that you can't wait to make.

Vary the colors depending on your personal preference. Turn the Red Cap Mushroom into another variety of mushroom, and the Jug crocheted in colors which match your kitchen.

Duckling in an Egg

Level of Difficulty
Beginner

Measurements
Approx 9 x 7.5 in
(23 x 19 cm)

Materials
Schachenmayr Catania
in White (color 106)
and Yellow (color 208),
100g each, Orange
(color 189), Black (color
110) and Azure (color
174), small amounts

Hook: US size C
(2.5 mm)

Embroidery needle

Gauge
18 sts and 20 rows =
4 x 4 in (10 x 10 cm)

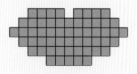

▨ = 1 sc in yellow
▨ = 1 sc in orange
☐ = 1 sc in white

Sc worked back and forth. Turn every row with ch 1.

Instructions

In white, ch 18 to turn, then follow the chart.

Beginning with the 2nd row carry the yellow strand along with the white. When changing colors, begin the sc with the old color (bring working yarn through loops of st below) and finish with new color through the two loops on hook. Hold strand of unused thread along the top of the previous row of sc and catch at each stitch of the new row.

With orange, follow chart for the beak. For the eyes, make an adjustable ring in black, with 7 sc. Close the ring by tightening the tail and sew on the eyes. With Azure, embroider the chain with chain st.

Finishing

Finish the potholder with 1 rnd of sc in the appropriate color. For the hanging loop, ch 15 in white and cover with sc.

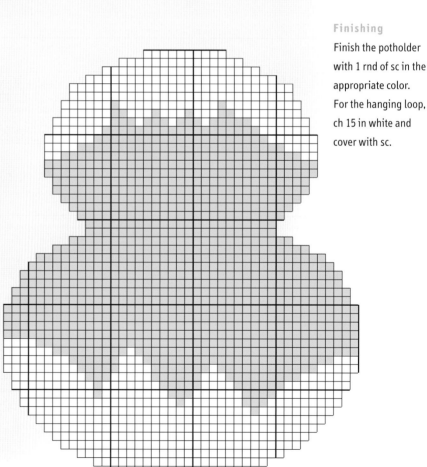

Cheerful Rabbit

Level of Difficulty
Beginner

Measurements
Approx 8 x 11 in
(20 x 28 cm)

Materials
Schachenmayer Catania in Chestnut (color 157) and Beige (color 108), 100g ea, White (color 106) and Black (color 110), remnants

Hook: US size C (2.5 mm)

Embroidery needle

Gauge
18 sts and 20 rows =
4 x 4 in (10 x 10 cm)

■ = 1 sc in Beige
■ = 1 sc in Chestnut
▥ = 1 sc in Black
☐ = 1 sc in White

Eyes   Teeth   Nose

Pattern Stitch
Sc worked back and forth. Turn every row with ch 1.

Instructions
Ch 33 (ch 10 in chestnut, ch 6 in beige, ch 10 in chestnut and ch 6 in beige) to turn. Work according to chart. When changing colors, begin the sc with the old color (bring working yarn through loops of st below) and finish with new color through the two loops on hook. Hold strand of unused thread along the top of the previous row of sc and catch at each stitch of the new row. Weave in the ends and work 1 rnd of sc in the appropriate color. For the eyes, follow the chart and work 2 ovals in white. For the pupils, in black, work 2 adjustable rings each with 8 hdc. Weave in the ends and sew on the white ovals. With black, follow chart for nose. With white, follow chart for teeth.

Finishing
Sew on the eyes, nose and teeth. Embroider the mouth in stem st. For the hanging loop between the ears, ch 12 in chestnut and work one rnd sc.

Stork

Level of Difficulty
Beginner

Measurements
Approx 8 ½ x 9 in
(22 x 23 cm)

Materials
Schachenmayr Catania
in Light Blue (color
173) and White (color
106), 100g each, Red
(color 115), 50g, Black
(color 110) and Rose
(color 158), small
amounts

Hook: US size C
(2.5 mm)

Gauge
18 sts and 20 rows =
4 x 4 in (10 x 10 cm)

Chart and Diagram
p 34

Pattern Stitch
Sc worked back and forth. Turn every row with ch 1.

Instructions
With light blue, ch 48 to turn and work following the chart on page 34. When changing colors, begin the sc with the old color (bring working yarn through loops of st below) and finish with new color through the two loops on hook. Hold strand of unused thread along the top of the previous row of sc and catch at each stitch of the new row (see Diagram page 34).

I recommend that when you get to the stork legs, you crochet the white and light blue strands together. In the light blue section between the red legs, the red and white strands will be joined.

Make sure that the yarns cross on the WS of the fabric when changing colors.

If you are stranding over more than 1 stitch, catch the unused thread on the WS. That way the back will look neater and there won't be any long strands of thread visible. If the distance to the next color change is too far, we recommend that you wind the pattern color thread onto a bobbin so that the surface of the potholder will not be uneven. In the section of the potholder with the motif, use small bobbins for each of the pattern colors.

Finishing
Weave in all tails. Finish the potholder with 1 rnd sc each in light blue and red and then 1 rnd "mouse-tooth" edging in red. For the hanging loop, ch 15 and cover with sc.

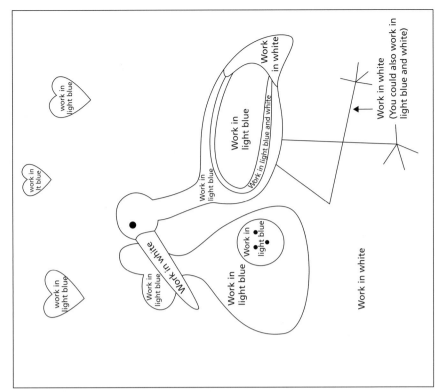

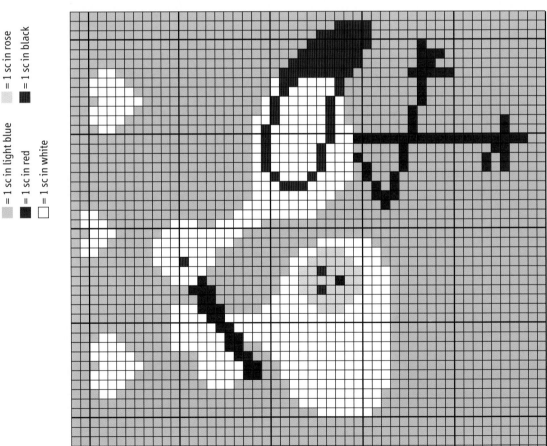

Work in white

Work in white
and black

Work in black

Work in white

Work in red and brown here

Work in white

Work in black and beige

Work in black

Work in white

Work in white

Work in white

Work in black

Work in white

Work in black and beige

Work in black and beige

Work in white

Work in black

Work in black

Work in white

Work in white

Work in black

Work in white

Work in white
and black

Work in black

Work in red and brown here

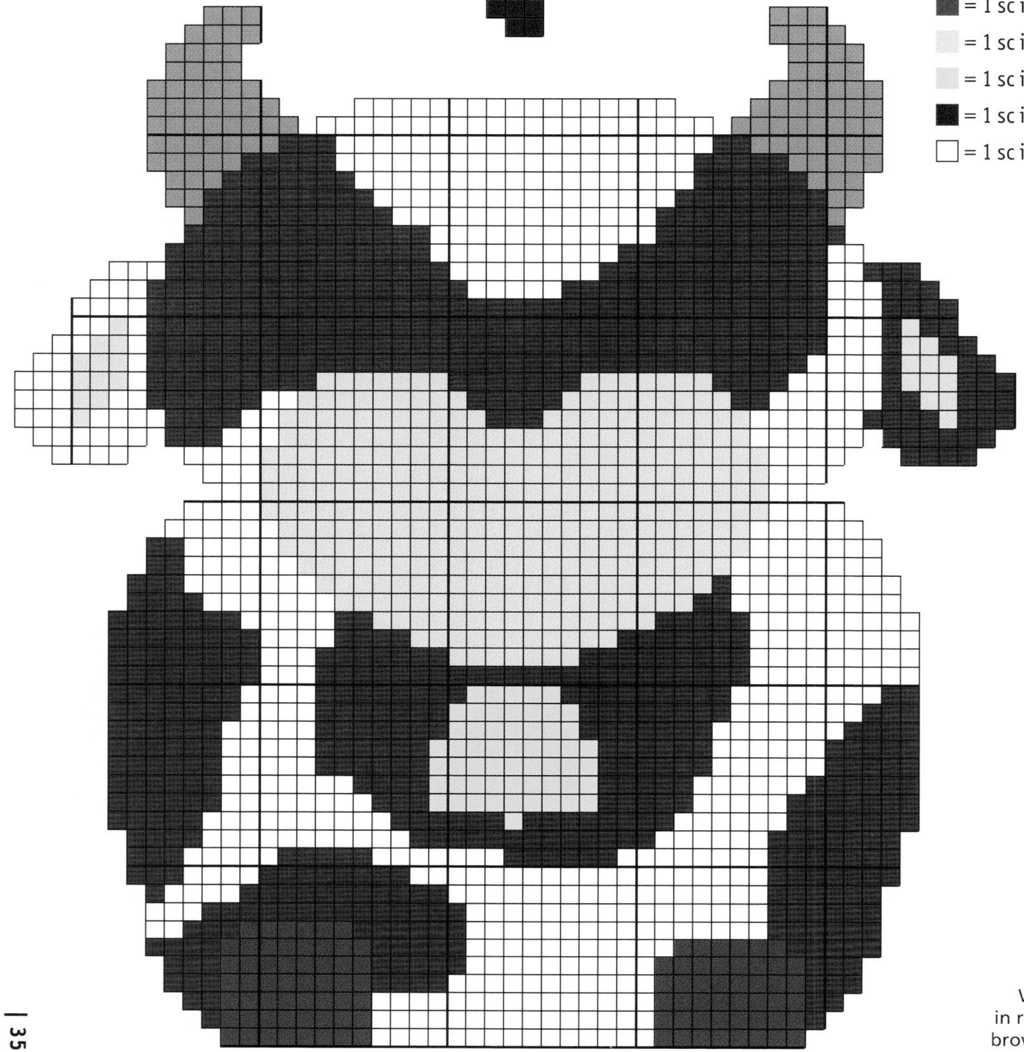

= 1 sc in black
= 1 sc in beige
= 1 sc in red-brown
= 1 sc in rose
= 1 sc in yellow
= 1 sc in pink
= 1 sc in white

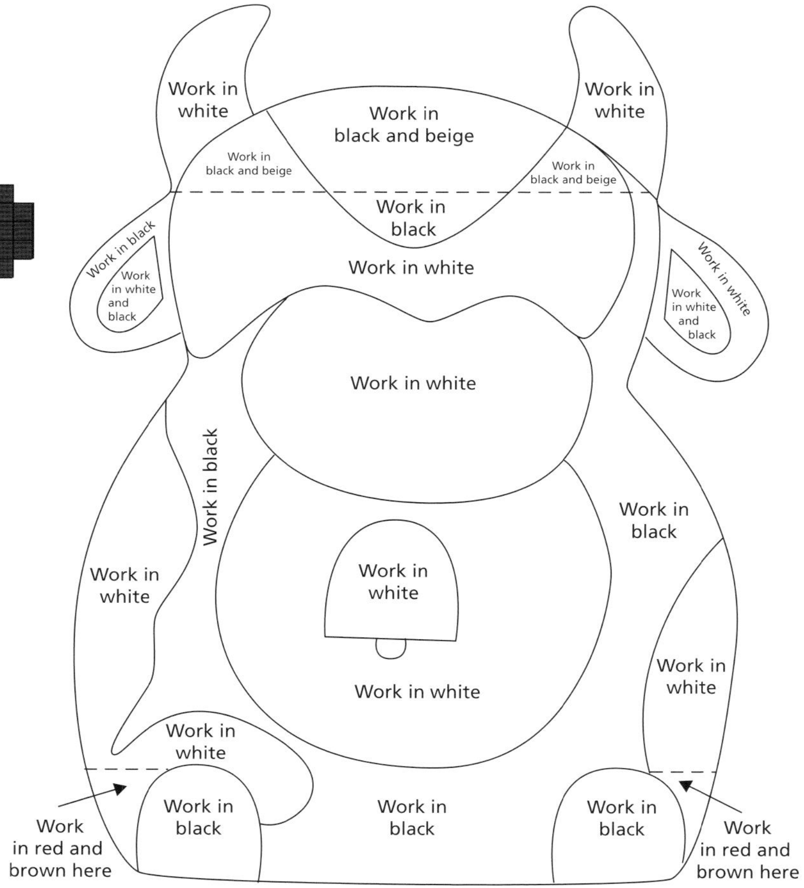

Nostril

Spotted Cow

Level of Difficulty
Intermediate

Measurements
Approx 8 x 10 in
(20 x 25 cm)

Materials
Schachenmayer
Catania in White (color
106) and Black (color
110), 100g each,
Rose (color 158), 50g,
Pink (color 223),
Royal (color 201),
Yellow (color 208),
Red-brown (color 210),
and Beige (color 108),
small amounts

Hook: US size C
(2.5 mm)

Embroidery needle

Gauge
18 sts and 20 rows =
4 x 4 in (10 x 10 cm)

Chart and Diagram
p 35

Pattern Stitch
Sc worked back and forth. Turn every row with ch 1.

Instructions
Ch 32 (ch 8 in red-brown, ch 15 in white and ch 8 in red-brown) to turn. Follow chart on p 35. When changing colors, begin the sc with the old color (bring working yarn through loops of st below) and finish with new color through the two loops on hook. Hold strand of unused thread along the top of the previous row of sc and catch at each stitch of the new row (see Diagram page 35). Work with 2 balls of black from the 22nd through the 34th row, as the area around the mouth is worked in white and to either side of the mouth, in black. Work with 3 balls of black from the 35th through the 37th row. In the 35th row, inc 8 sts on each side, but for the black ear, add the 8 ch sts at the end of the 34th row. For the white ear, add the 8 ch sts at the 35th row as shown in the chart. Work the 33rd and 34th rows of the ears later in their respective colors. Attach a new white strand for the last couple of rows on the top part of the head.

Finishing
Weave in all ends and finish the potholder with 1 rnd sc in the appropriate color. Follow the chart and work the nostrils in pink. Make two adjustable rings in Royal for the eyes with 12 dc and sew them on. Embroider stem st, with white, the contour of the legs, and with black, the mouth. For the hanging loop, ch 12 with white and cover with 1 rnd sc.

Good Kitchen Ghost

Level of Difficulty
Beginner

Measurements
Approx 7 ½ x 10 in
(19 x 25 cm)

Materials
Schachenmayer Cata-
nia in White (color
106), 100g and Black
(color 110), remnant

Hook: US size C
(2.5 mm)

Embroidery needle

Gauge
18 sts and 20 rows =
4 x 4 in (10 x 10 cm)

Pattern Stitch
Sc worked back and forth. Turn every row with ch 1.

Instructions
With white, ch 34 to turn and follow chart.

Work with a double strand of white so that the potholder will be more durable.

Finish the little tail on the side at the 19th row on and then for the body, re-attach the yarn. Work the ghost in one piece up to the 28th row. From the 29th row on, work the right arm only, then re-attach a new strand to complete the left arm. Finally, work the head. Weave in all ends. With white, work around ghost once in sc.

Finishing
For the hanging loop, on the back at the 47th row and a distance of about ½ in from the edges, ch 12 with white join to form ring, 12 sc into round. Work mouth and nose in black following the chart and sew on. For the eyes, make two adjustable rings in black with 10 hdc and sew on.

▨ = 1sc in black

☐ = 1 sc in white

▬ = 1 sl st in black

Mouth   Nose

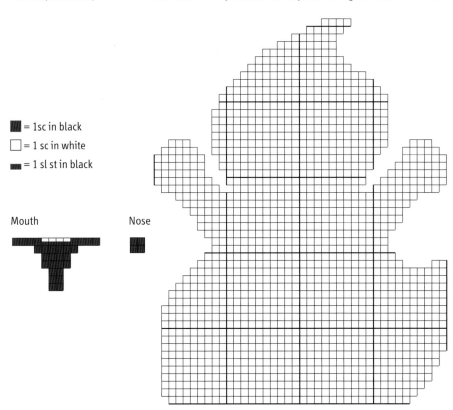

Spider in the Web

Level of Difficulty
Intermediate

Measurements
Approx 7 ½ in (19 cm)
in diameter

Materials
Schachenmayer Cata-
nia in White (color
106), 100g and Black
(color 110), small
amount

Hook: US size C
(2.5 cm)

Blunt-tipped yarn
needle

Magic Pen

Gauge
18 sts and 20 rows =
4 x 4 in (10 x 10 cm)

Pattern Stitch
Sc in the rnd, beginning each rnd with an sc 1 and ending each rnd with 1 sl st.

Instructions
Rnd 1: With white, make an adjustable ring, 8 sc in ring.

Rnds 2-3: Sc around, increasing in every other st.

Rnd 4: Sc around, increasing in every 3rd st.

Rnd 5: Sc around, increasing in every 4th st.

Rnd 6: Sc around, increasing in the 2nd and then in every 5th st 5 times.

Rnd 7: Sc around, increasing in every 6th st.

Rnd 8: Sc around, increasing in the 3rd st and then in every 7th st 5 times.

Rnd 9: Sc around, increasing in every 8th st.

Rnd 10: Sc around, increasing in the 4th st and then in every 9th st 5 times.

Rnd 11: Sc around, increasing in every 10th st.

Rnd 12: Sc around, increasing in the 5th st and then in every 11th st 5 times.

Rnd 13: Sc around, increasing in every 12th st.

Rnd 14: Sc around, increasing in the 6th st and then in every 13th st 5 times.

Rnd 15: Sc around, increasing in every 14th st.

Rnd 16: Sc around, increasing in the 7th and then in every 15th st 5 times.

Rnd 17: Sc around, increasing in every 16th st.

Rnd 18: Sc around, increasing in the 8th st and then in every 17th st 5 times.

Rnd 19: Sc around, increasing in every 18th st.

Rnd 20: Sc around, increasing in the 9th st and then in every 19th st 5 times.

Rnd 21: Sc around, increasing in every 20th st.

Rnd 22: Sc around, increasing in the 10th st and then in every 21st st 5 times.

Rnd 23: Sc around, increasing in every 22nd st.

Rnd 24: Sc around, increasing in the 11th st and then in every 23rd st 5 times.

For the last round, work the hanging loop with white: ch 12 and cover chain loop with sc.

= 1 sc in black

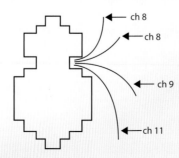

ch 8

ch 8

ch 9

ch 11

Finishing
For the spider web, draw the lines with Magic Pen and then embroider them in stem stitch with black crochet thread. With black, crochet the spider following the chart below. Make the legs with chain and slip sts (see Diagram) and sew legs at spider's middle as shown. Sew the spider and its legs to the potholder. Use white crochet thread to make a cross on the spider's back.

Little Pumpkin Man

Level of Difficulty
Beginner

Measurements
Approx 6 ¾ x 9 ½ in
(17 x 24 cm)

Materials
Schachenmayr Catania
in Orange (color 189),
100g, Spring Green
(color 170), Chestnut
(color 157), White (col-
or 106), Red (color 115),
and Black (color 110),
small amounts

Hook: US size C
(2.5 mm)

Gauge
18 sts and 20 rows =
4 x 4 in (10 x 10 cm)

Pattern Stitch
Sc worked back and forth. Turn every row with ch 1.

Instructions
With orange, ch 29 to turn and work following the chart. Use orange thread to join other parts of the potholder. When changing colors, make sure the colors always cross on the WS of the piece. Finish the little pumpkin man with a round of sc in orange; crochet his hands with spring green and the hat with chestnut. For the hanging loop, ch 12 with chestnut and cover loop with sc.

Crochet the eyes with three strands* of white held together. Work in sc following the chart. For the pupils and both buttons on the stomach, make a ring with black and cover with 8 sc using 3 strands of thread held together. Sew the pupils onto the whites of the eyes.

Make the mouth with 3 strands of red held together, following the chart. For the nose, make a ring with orange and cover with 9 sc. Finish the nose with 1 rnd sl st using 3 strands of red held together.

Finishing
Sew on the eyes, nose, mouth, and buttons. Embroi-der teeth onto the mouth with 3 strands of white held together. Draw the contour lines with magic pen and then embroider in stem stitch with 3 strands of brown held together.

*To get the three strands of thread, split the plies of the yarn into the desired number of strands; other-wise it will be too thick for the crochet and embroi-dery work.

Eye

Mouth

■ = 1 in orange
■ = 1 in chestnut
■ = 1 in spring green
■ = 1 in red
□ = 1 white

Red Cap Mushroom

Level of Difficulty
Beginner

Measurements
Approx 7 ½ x 9 in
(19 x 23 cm)

Materials
Schachenmayr Catania
in White (color 106),
100g and Red (color
115), 50 g

Hook: US size C
(2.5 mm)

Gauge
18 sts and 20 rows =
4 x 4 in (10 x 10 cm)

Pattern Stitch
Sc worked back and forth. Turn every row with ch 1.

Instructions
Ch 29 to turn. Follow chart.

Work the stalk of the mushroom with a double strand of white so that the potholder will be more durable.

While working the red cap, carry the white and while working the white dots, carry the red. Work the color changes as in Dutch Boys (page 14).

Finishing
Weave in the ends. Work 1 rnd of sc in the appropriate color. For the hanging loop, ch 12 in red and cover with 1 rnd sc.

■ = 1 sc in red
□ = 1 sc in white

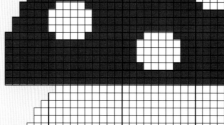

Four-cornered Star

Level of Difficulty
Beginner

Measurements
Approx 10.5 x 10.5 in
(26 x 26 cm)

Materials
Schachenmayr Catania
in White (color 106),
100g, Peacock (color
146), 50 g and Red
(color 115), small
amounts

Hook: US size C
(2.5 mm)

Gauge
18 sts and 20 rows =
4 x 4 in (10 x 10 cm)

Chart and Diagram
p 48

Pattern Stitch
Sc worked back and forth. Turn every row with ch 1.

Center Square
Row 1: Ch 18 to turn in peacock.
Rows 2-17: Work back and forth in sc. Cut yarn and weave in end.

Corners
Row 1: With white, sc 17 across 1 side of the square.
Rows 2-17: Ch 1 to turn, skip the 1st st of previous row and then work 1 sc in each of rem sts across. At the end of the row, be sure to work the last st. See chart p 48. Work the other 3 points of the star as for the 1st.

Finishing
With peacock, work 1 rnd of sc. At every tip work 3 sc into 1 st. Then work 16 sc into the valley (low point) then 16 sc to next tip. Continue with 1 rnd sc with white, 1 rnd with peacock, one with red, one peacock and finish 1 rnd with white. At the tip of each point, work 3 sc into the center sc of the previous rnd. For the hanging loop, ch 12 and cover with sc.

■ = 1 sc in peacock
□ = 1 sc in white

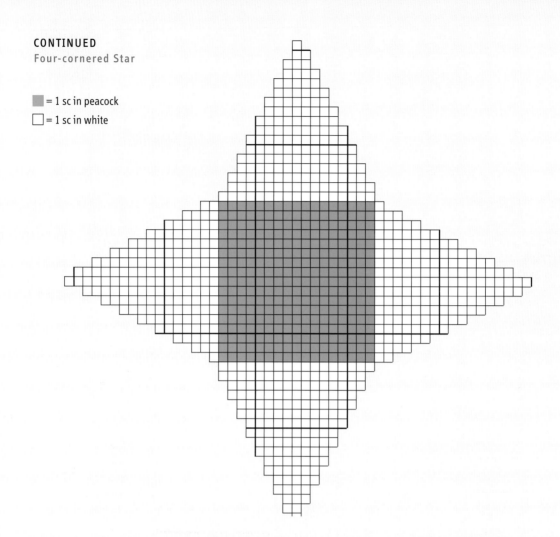

Santa Claus

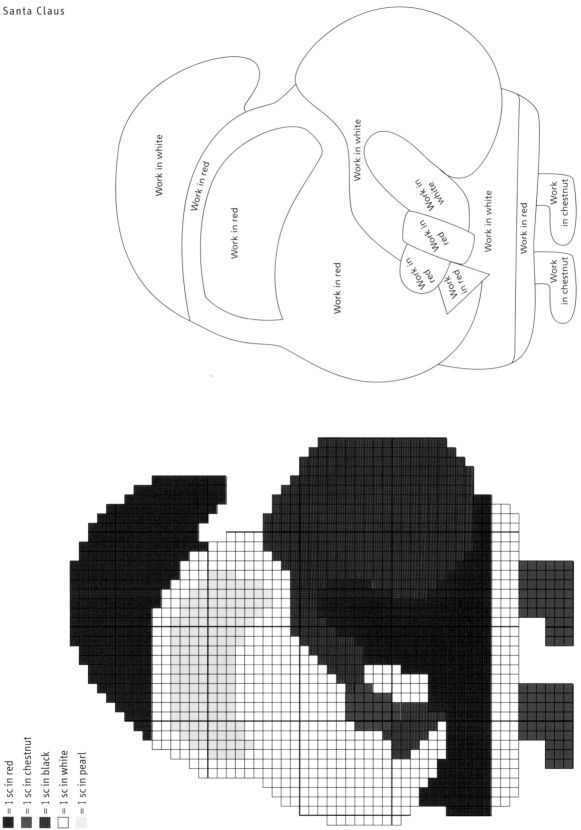

■ = 1 sc in red
▨ = 1 sc in chestnut
▨ = 1 sc in black
□ = 1 sc in white
▨ = 1 sc in pearl

Work in white
Work in red
Work in red
Work in white
Work in red
Work in white
Work in white
Work in red
Work in chestnut
Work in chestnut
Work in red
Work in red
Work in red
Work in red

Santa Claus

Level of Difficulty
Intermediate

Measurements
Approx 7 ½ x 10 ½ in
(19 x 26 cm)

Materials
Schachenmayr Catania
in White (color 106),
Red (color 115) and
Black (color 110), 50 g
each, Pearl (color 155)
and Chestnut (color
157), small amounts

Hook: US size C
(2.5 mm)

Blunt-tipped embroi-
dery needle

Embroidery needle

Gauge
18 sts and 20 rows =
4 x 4 in (10 x 10 cm)

Chart and Diagram
p 49

Pattern Stitch
Sc worked back and forth. Turn every row with ch 1.

Instructions
With white, ch 31 to turn. Beginning at bottom of Santa's jacket, work following the chart on p. 49.
Join in red at row 4. When changing colors, begin the sc with the old color (bring working yarn
through loops of st below) and finish with new color through the two loops on hook. Hold strand
of unused thread along the top of the previous row of sc and catch at each stitch of the new row
(see Diagram p. 49). On row 26 and the last 3 rows of Santa's sack, work with a separate strand of
black. On row 36, increase 7 sts for the cap. For the cap's pompon, finish rows 33-35 first. Finish by
crocheting Santa's boots with chestnut.
The chestnut–colored boots are attached after the Santa is complete. Stabilize each boot by joining
(or working) an additional strand of chestnut.
Weave in all tails and then crochet around Santa with 1 rnd sc in the same colors as for each potholder section. Make the nose with an adjustable ring with red and cover with 10 hdc. Make an
adjustable ring with black and 8 sc for each eye and another adjustable ring in white covered with
12 dc for the cap's pompon.

Finishing
Sew on the eyes and nose; attach pompon to point of cap. Embroider the mouth and underarms with
stem stitch in red. For the hanging loop, ch 12 with red and cover loop with sc.

1001 Nights

Level of Difficulty
Intermediate

Measurements
Approx 9 x 4 ½ in
(23 x 12 cm)

Materials
Schachenmayr Catania
in Azure (color 174),
100g and Red (color
115), 50 g

Anchor Artistic Metallic
in Gold (color 300),
small amount

Hook: US size C
(2.5 mm)

Gauge
18 sts and 20 rows =
4 x 4 in (10 x 10 cm)

**Chart A and Dia-
grams B and C
p 54**

Pattern Stitch

Dc in the rnd, beginning every rnd with ch 1 and ending with sl st.

Instructions

Crochet 4 squares in azure and 1 square in red. See chart A. Sew the squares together in sc with the gold thread as described in diagrams B and C. Pay close attention to the order of the numbers. First, following diagram B, sew together the underside of the slipper. Then, following diagram C, work the top of the slipper.

Finishing

For the hanging loop, ch 25 in gold and cover with 2 rows sc. Decorate the slipper as desired, either with bead embroidery or a tassel, as shown.

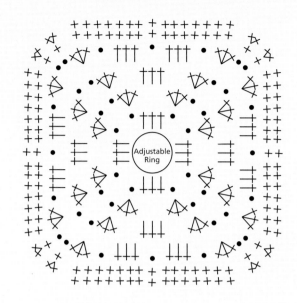

Chart A

Squares in Red and Azure

$+$ = sc

● = ch

○ = sl st

⋉ = 2 sc into 1 st

⋈ = 3 sc into 1 st

† = dc

Diagram B

Assemble underside of slipper

Begin at the heel part of the sole (point A) and end at point B. Crochet all pieces together following the pattern by working 2 sc in each of the 4 corner sts.

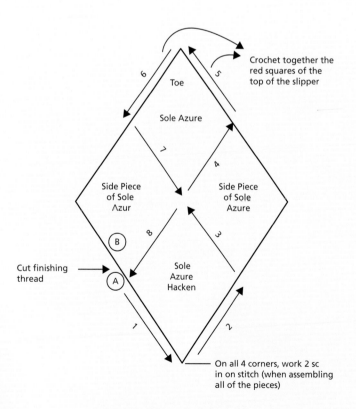

Crochet together the red squares of the top of the slipper

Toe

Sole Azure

6

5

7

4

Side Piece of Sole Azur

Side Piece of Sole Azure

B

8

3

A

Sole Azure Hacken

Cut finishing thread

1

2

On all 4 corners, work 2 sc in on stitch (when assembling all of the pieces)

Diagram C

Assemble top of slipper

Connect all pieces with sc. Begin at point A and end at point B. Then begin at point C and work to point D. Work the side pieces marked ⓧ and ⓨ. Together with 1 sl st continue closing up to point E and stop. Work 2 sc in 1st at each of 4 corners.

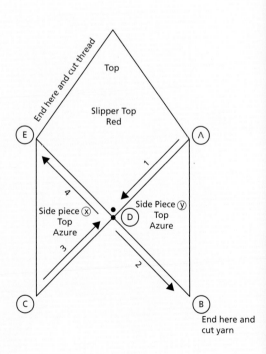

End here and cut thread

Top

Slipper Top Red

E

∧

1

4

Side piece ⓧ Top Azure

D

Side Piece ⓨ Top Azure

3

2

C

B

End here and cut yarn

Little Dress Potholder

Chart

● = ch

† = tr

Skip 14 treble pairs

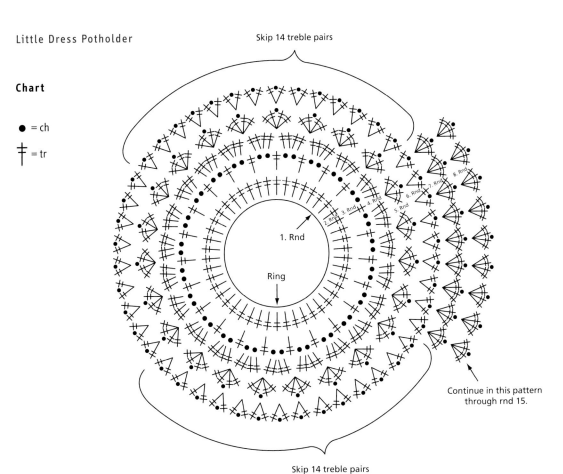

1. Rnd

Ring

2. Rnd 3. Rnd 4. Rnd 5. Rnd 6. Rnd 7. Rnd 8. Rnd

Continue in this pattern
through rnd 15.

Skip 14 treble pairs

Diagram

Work is joined at these points to form the skirt

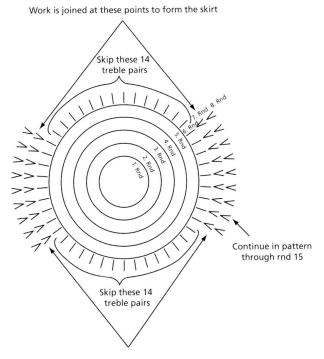

Skip these 14
treble pairs

7. Rnd 8. Rnd
6. Rnd
5. Rnd
4. Rnd
3. Rnd
2. Rnd
1. Rnd

Continue in pattern
through rnd 15

Skip these 14
treble pairs

Work is joined at these points to form the skirt

Little Dress Potholder

Level of Difficulty
Intermediate

Measurements
Approx 7 x 8 in
(17 x 20 cm)

Materials
Schachenmayr Catania
in Red (color 115), 100
g and White (color
106), 50g

Hook: US size C
(2.5 mm)

Gauge
18 sts and 20 rows =
4 x 4 in (10 x 10 cm)

Chart and Diagram
p 55

Pattern Stitch
Dc in the rnd, beginning every rnd with ch 1 and ending with sl st.

Instructions
See Diagram p. 55.

The trebles are not worked into the stitches of the previous round but around the trebles and chains of the previous round.

Rnd 1: With white, Make an adjustable ring.

Rnd 2: 46 tr into ring.

Rnd 3, with red: In every other tr, work 1 tr, ch 2.

Rnd 4, with white: 4 tr into every chain loop around.

Rnd 5, with red: In the spaces between every 4 tr group, work 4 tr with ch 1 between the 2nd and 3rd trebles.

Rnd 6, with white: In the spaces between every 4 tr group and in the chain between the 2nd and 3rd tr of the previous rnd, work 2 tr, with ch 1 between each tr pair.

Rnd 7: For the red dress, in the ch st of the next 9 consecutive tr pairs, work 4 tr with ch 1 between the 2nd and 3rd tr. Skip the next 14 tr pairs and, in each ch st of the 15th-23rd pairs, work 4 tr with ch 1 between the 2nd and 3rd tr. Skip another 14 pairs and finish the round with a sl st into beginning tr.

Color Sequence
Rnd 8-11 and 14-15: Red.

Rnd 12-13: White.

Rnds 8-15: ^In the chain st between the 2nd and 3rd tr of previous rnd, work 4 tr with ch 1 between the 2nd and 3rd tr; rep from * around.

Finishing
With white, work 1 rnd of "mouse-tooth" edging around the bottom of the dress. Work hanging loop across back neck of dress with red: ch 12 and cover with sc. With white, use slip and chain sts to make a tie around the waist of the dress.

Colorful Jug

Level of Difficulty
Intermediate

Measurements
Approx 7 ½ x 6 ½ in
(19 x 16 cm)

Materials
Schachenmayr Catania
in Light Blue (color
173), Red (color 115),
White (color 106),
Spring Green (color
170), and Yellow (color
208), small amounts

Hook: US size C
(2.5 mm)

Gauge
18 sts and 20 rows =
4 x 4 in (10 x 10 cm)

Chart
p 60

Pattern Stitch

Sc in the rnd, beginning every rnd with ch 1 and ending with sl st.

Instructions

Work following the chart on page 60 and color sequence below.

Rnd 1: With light blue, ch 18 to turn. Sc across top and bottom of chain = 34 sc total.

Rnds 2-3: Sc around.

Rnd 4: Sc around, increasing at each side (in the 1st and 17th sts) = 36 sts.

Rnds 5-11: Sc around, increasing at each side on every rnd = 50 sts.

Rnds 12-13: Sc around.

Rnds 14-15: Sc around, increasing at each side on each rnd = 54 sts.

Rnd 16: Sc with red, working 3 sc into st at each side = 58 sts.

Rnds 17-23: Sc around, increasing at each side on every rnd = 72 sts.

Rnds 24-30: Sc around.

Rnd 31: Sc around, decreasing 1 st at each side = 70 sts.

Rnd 32: Sc around.

Rnd 33: Sc around, decreasing 1 st at spout side only = 69 sts.

Rnd 34: Sc around.

Rnd 35: Sc around, decreasing 1 st at each side = 67 sts.

Rnd 36: Sc around.

Rnd 37: Sc around, decreasing 1 st at same side as on rnd 33 = 66 sts.

Rnds 38-42: Sc around.

Rnd 43: Sc around, increasing at spout side only = 67 sts.

Rnd 44: Sc around, increasing 2 sts at spout side = 69 sts.

Rnd 45: Sc around, increasing 3 sts evenly spaced at spout = 72 sts.

Rnd 46: Sc around.

Rnd 47: Sc around, increasing 4 sts evenly spaced at spout = 76 sts.

Rnds 48-49: Sc around, increasing 5 sts evenly spaced at spout on each rnd = 86 sts.

At the spout side on rnds 44, 45, and 47, increases are worked in every other st and on rnds 48 and 49, increases are on every 3rd st. Do not place increases directly above one another, or the spout will not be nicely shaped.

Color Sequence

Rnds 1-9: Light Blue

Rnds 10-11: White

Rnds 12-13: Alternate 2 sts White and 2 sts Light Blue

Rnds 14-15: White

Rnds 16-22: Red

Rnds 23-25: Spring Green

Rnds 26-28: Patterned in spring green and white (see chart)

Rnds 29-31: Spring Green

Rnds 32-35: White

Rnds 36-37: Yellow

Rnds 38-40: Red

Rnds 41-42: Yellow

Rnds 43-44: Spring Green

Rnds 44-45: White

Rnds 47-49: Red

Finishing

For the handle, ch 20 with red and then sc along both sides of the chain, working 3 sc into one st at each end of the handle. At the same time, when working the lower end of the handle, attach it with 2 sc to the body of the jug at the first yellow rnd (rnd 36). Join [eliminate the] 2 sc of the upper end of the handle to [eliminate the] 2 sc on the second-to-last row of the jug. Now, with yellow, work 1 row of sc around handle, joining with 3 sc where the handle meets jug at rnd 35 (that is, on the row below the previous join). Finish the top edge of the jug with 1 rnd sc in yellow. At the same time, join the top row of the handle to top row of jug with about 4 sc.

Note: The stitch count in the drawing does not match that of the actual jug. For correct stitch count, please consult the text above. The drawing only shows the color sequence and the rate of increase.

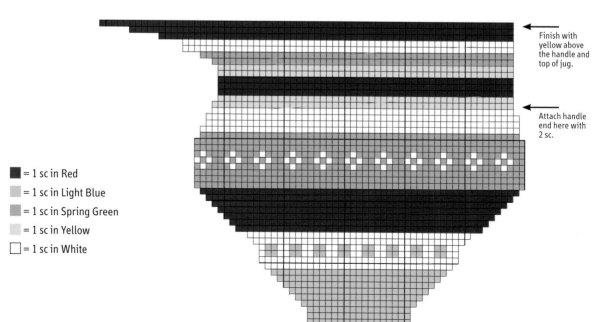

Finish with yellow above the handle and top of jug.

Attach handle end here with 2 sc.

■ = 1 sc in Red

▨ = 1 sc in Light Blue

▨ = 1 sc in Spring Green

▨ = 1 sc in Yellow

□ = 1 sc in White

BLOSSOM AND ROSETTE POTHOLDERS

STRIKING BLOSSOMS AND ROSETTES ON PRACTICAL POT-HOLDERS! In pastels, and classic potholder colors, blossoms and rosettes are everywhere.

You'll find both challenging designs, like the rose or the pot-holder with pastel flowers as well as more simple designs like the heart and the colorful blossoms.

These vintage potholders are wonderfully eye-catching, and not seen all that often in kitchens anymore. It's just one more reason to get started making blossoms, filigree and rosettes.

Spiral with Blossoms

Level of Difficulty
Intermediate

Measurements
Approx 8 in (20 cm)

Materials
Schachenmayer Catania in White (color 106) and Red (color 115), 100g

Hook: US size C (2.5 mm)

Blunt-tipped embroidery needle

Gauge
18 sts and 20 rows = 4 x 4 in (10 x 10 cm)

Chart A and Diagram B p 64

Pattern Stitch

The center is worked in double crochet as a spiral. Place a contrast color strand between the sts where the rnd ends to keep track of stitch counts. 12 sts are increased on each round; work increases with 2 sts into 1.

Center Section

Rnd 1: Make an adjustable ring, 12 dc in ring, closing ring with 1 sl st.

From this point, the potholder is worked as a spiral!

Rnd 2: Increase 1 in every st around.
Rnd 3: Increase in every other st around (the 3rd rnd begins at the 12th increase of the 2nd rnd).
Rnd 4: Increase in every 3rd st around.
Rnd 5: Increase in every 4th st around.
Rnd 6: Increase in every 5th st around.
Rnd 7: Increase in every 6th st around.
Rnd 8: Increase in every 7th st around.
To make a smooth transition at the end of the last rnd, work last increase as 3 dc, 1 hdc, 1 sc, 1 sl st. After completing rnd 8, cut yarn and begin rnd 9 at another place on the potholder, not at the previous rnd beginning.
Rnd 9: Sc around, increasing 3 sts evenly spaced around.

Blossoms

See Chart A, p. 64.
Rnd 1: With white, ch 6 and join into ring with sl st.
Rnd 2: 12 sc around ring.
Rnd 3: With red, 1 sc into every other st of previous rnd and ch 1 between each sc.
Rnd 4: In every chain st, make 1 sc, 3 dc, 1 sc to form a petal. The first blossom is joined to the potholder center on the second-to-last and last petals with a sl st after the first dc (of group of 3). Finish the 3rd dc and the sc of final petal and cut yarn.
When working all subsequent blossoms, join the third petal to the previous petal with 1 sl st and join the second-to-last and last petals to the center section of the potholder with a sl st at each join. The potholder and blossom petals are connected on every 4th sc of the potholder center with 1 sl st (see Diagram B, p. 64).

Finishing

Weave in ends and make a hanging loop with red: ch 12 and cover loop with sc. Finish by embroidering spiral in red and stem stitch, following the rounds as shown.

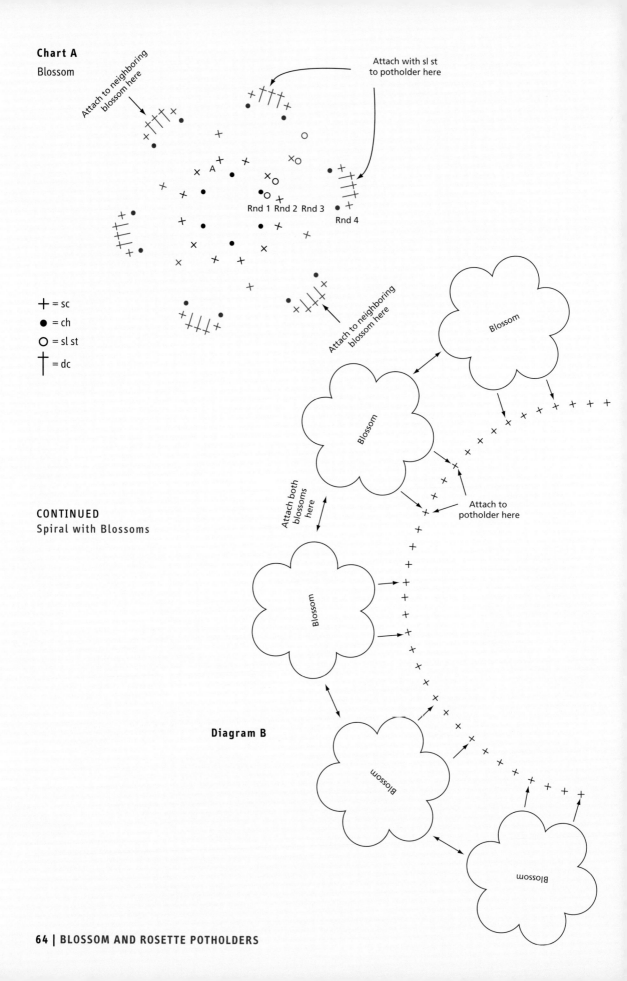

Attach to neighboring
blossom here

Attach with sl st
to potholder here

A

Rnd 1 Rnd 2 Rnd 3
Rnd 4

$+$ = sc

● = ch

O = sl st

$\dagger$ = dc

Attach to neighboring
blossom here

Blossom

Blossom

Attach to
potholder here

CONTINUED
Spiral with Blossoms

Attach both
blossoms
here

Blossom

Blossom

Diagram B

Blossom

Blossom

Diagram D

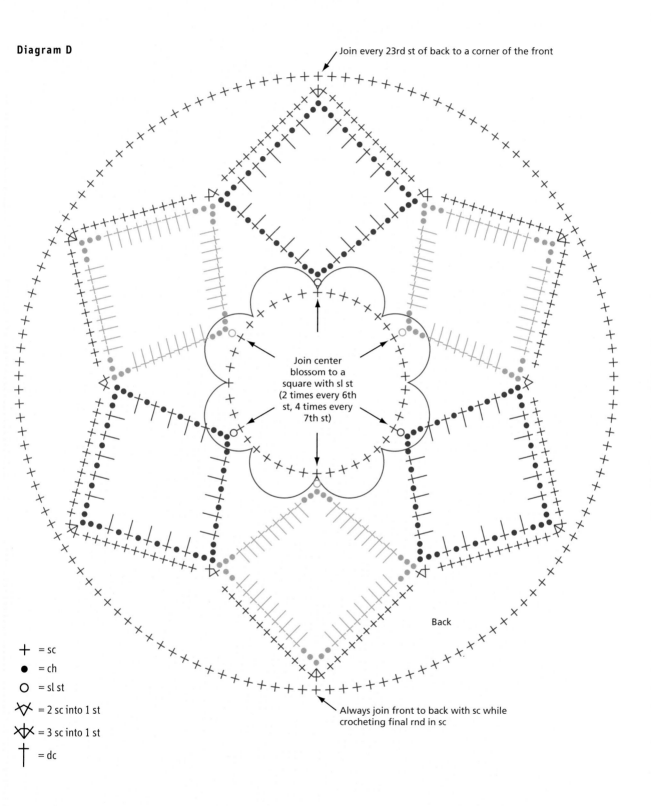

Join every 23rd st of back to a corner of the front

Join center blossom to a square with sl st (2 times every 6th st, 4 times every 7th st)

Back

Always join front to back with sc while crocheting final rnd in sc

$+$ = sc

$\bullet$ = ch

$\bigcirc$ = sl st

$\times\!\!\!\!\vee$ = 2 sc into 1 st

$\times\!\!\!\!\vee\!\!\!\!\times$ = 3 sc into 1 st

$\dagger$ = dc

Blossom and Squares

Level of Difficulty
Experienced

Measurements
Approx 8 ¾ in (22 cm)

Materials
Schachenmayr Catania in White (color 106), 100 g, Azure (color 174), Red (color 115), and Melon (color 235), small amounts

Hook: US size C (2.5 mm)

Gauge
18 sts and 20 rows = 4 x 4 in (10 x 10 cm)

Chart and Diagram
Diagram D, p 65
Chart A, p 68
Charts B and C, p 69

Pattern Stitch
Sc and dc worked in the round; begin each rnd with ch 1 and end with 1 sl st.

Instructions

Back (worked in sc with white)

Rnd 1: Make an adjustable ring, 8 sc in ring.

Rnds 2-3: Increase in every other st around.

Rnd 4: Increase in every 3rd st around.

Rnd 5: Increase in every 4th st around.

Rnd 6: Increase in the 2nd st and then (increase in every 5th st) 5 times.

Rnd 7: Increase in every 6th st around.

Rnd 8: Increase in the 3rd st and then (increase in every 7th st) 5 times.

Rnd 9: Increase in every 8th st around.

Rnd 10: Increase in the 4th st and then (increase in every 9th st) 5 times.

Rnd 11: Increase in every 10th st around.

Rnd 12: Increase in the 5th st and then (increase in every 11th st) 5 times.

Rnd 13: Increase in every 12th st around.

Rnd 14: Increase in the 6th st and then (increase in every 13th st) 5 times.

Rnd 15: Increase in every 14th st around.

Rnd 16: Increase in the 7th st and then (increase in every 15th st) 5 times.

Rnd 17: Increase in every 16th st around.

Rnd 18: Increase in the 8th st and then (increase in every 17th st) 5 times.

Rnd 19: Increase in every 18th st around.

Rnd 20: Increase in the 9th st and then (increase in every 19th st) 5 times.

Rnd 21: Increase in every 20th st around.

Rnd 22: Increase in the 10th st and then (increase in every 21st st) 5 times.

Rnd 23: Increase in every 22nd st around.

Front Blossom

See Chart A, p. 68

Rnd 1: With red, make an adjustable ring, 24 dc in ring.

Rnd 2: 1 sc in each dc of round below.

Rnd 3: Sc around, increasing in every 3rd st.

Rnd 4: Sc around, increasing in every 4th st.

Rnd 5: *In first sc of previous rnd, work 1 sc, 1 hdc, 1 dc; 1 tr into each of the next two sc; in the next sc, work 1 dc, 1 hdc, 1 sc; skip 1 sc. Repeat from * around.

Melon Square

See Chart B, p. 69.

Rnd 1: Ch 4 and join into ring.

Rnd 2: *3 dc, ch 2; rep from * 3 more times.

Rnd 3: *2 dc; (2 dc, ch 3, 2 dc) into corner (the ch 2 loop of rnd below); rep from * around.

Rnd 4: *5 dc, (2 dc, ch 5, 2 dc) into corner (the ch 3 loop of rnd below); rep from * around.

Azure Square

See Chart C, p. 69.

Rnd 1: Ch 4 and join into ring.

Rnd 2: *3 dc, ch 2; rep from * 3 more times.

Rnd 3: *2 dc; (2 dc, ch 3, 2 dc) into corner (the ch 2 loop of rnd below); rep from * around.

Rnd 4: *1 dc, ch 1, 1 dc, ch 1, 1 dc, ch 1, then (1 dc, ch 5, 1 dc) into corner (the ch 3 loop of rnd below); rep from * around.

Each square is joined at the last corner of the 4th rnd to the center blossom (see Diagram D, p. 65). Equally space the squares around the blossom. Make the join on the last rnd with sc (4th rnd) to the back of the blossom working a sc into the chain. Work the last 2 ch of the corner and then finish the square (see Charts B and C).

Join the squares with a sc in red (see Diagram D) by working 1 sc into each st of the 4th rnd of the squares. At the conjunctions between the squares, skip 1 ch per square. This point will later be joined to the back with 3 sc in the center of the 5 chain loop of the outer corner.

At the conjunction between 2 squares, sc in the first ch of the corner, skip 1 ch, go into the 3rd ch st and pull 1 loop through without finishing the stitch. Instead, go into the ch 3 loop of the joined adjacent squares, pull 1 loop through, and join the single crochets together. Skip 1 ch of the previous row of the adjacent square and then work 1 sc into the ch 5 loop of the corner. Continue in the same manner around (see Diagram D)

Chart A

Center Blossom

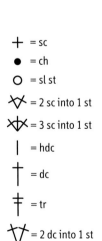

+ = sc

● = ch

○ = sl st

⅄ = 2 sc into 1 st

Ⅹ⅄ = 3 sc into 1 st

| = hdc

† = dc

‡ = tr

∨ = 2 dc into 1 st

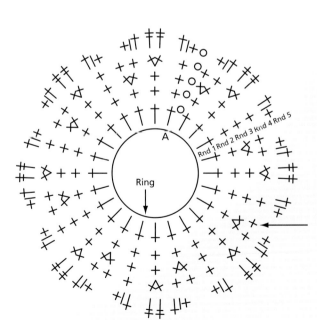

Rnd 1 Rnd 2 Rnd 3 Rnd 4 Rnd 5

A

Ring

Finishing

Weave in all ends. Join the back of the potholder to the front with 1 rnd sc in red. Join at every 23rd st of the back with a center corner sc of a square (see Diagram D). Finish the potholder with a "mouse-tooth" edging and make a hanging loop: ch 12 with red and cover with sc.

Chart B

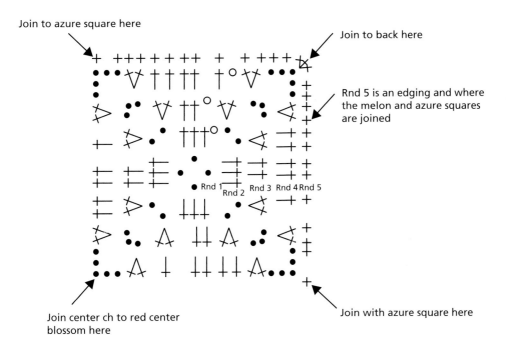

Join to azure square here

Join to back here

Rnd 5 is an edging and where the melon and azure squares are joined

Rnd 1 Rnd 2 Rnd 3 Rnd 4 Rnd 5

Join center ch to red center blossom here

Join with azure square here

Chart C

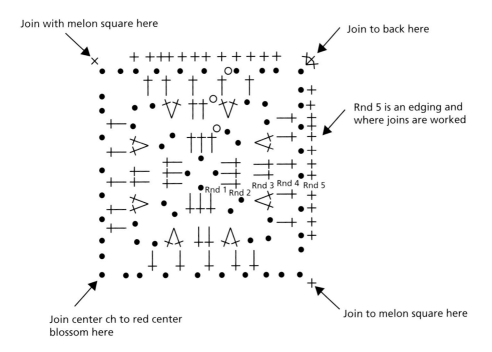

Join with melon square here

Join to back here

Rnd 5 is an edging and where joins are worked

Rnd 1 Rnd 2 Rnd 3 Rnd 4 Rnd 5

Join center ch to red center blossom here

Join to melon square here

Gyro Pattern

Level of Difficulty
Intermediate

Measurements
Approx 8 in (20 cm)

Materials
Schachenmayr Catania
in Maroon (color 157)
and Pearl (color 155),
100 g each

Hook: US size C
(2.5 mm)

Gauge
18 sts and 20 rows =
4 x 4 in (10 x 10 cm)

Pattern Stitch

Spiral and joined rounds in sc. Begin joined rnds with ch 1 and end with 1 sl st.

Instructions

On the two-color rounds of this potholder, catch the unused color on each stitch as you work around (see Dutch Boys, p. 14).

Rnd 1: Make an adjustable ring with maroon, 12 sc in ring; join with sl st.

Rnd 2: Begin working in sc as a spiral, alternating maroon and pearl, catching unused color with each st. Begin with maroon and alternate 2 sc with maroon and 2 sc with pearl, working 2 sc into each st around = 24 sts.

When changing colors begin sc with old color and bring new color through the two loops on hook.

Rnd 3: 1 sc into each st around. Begin with 3 sc maroon and then alternate 2 sc with each color. End rnd with 3 sc pearl. The last stitch is the transition to the next rnd.

Rnd 4: Increase in every other st. Alternate 3 sc in each color around, ending with 4 sc pearl. On the 3rd sc of the last pearl segment, work 2 sc into 1 st.

Rnd 5: Increase in every 3rd st around. Alternate 4 sc in each color, ending with 5 sc pearl. On the 4th sc of the last pearl segment, work 2 sc into 1 st.

Rnd 6: Increase in every 4th st around. Alternate 5 sc in each color, ending with 5 sc pearl. On the last pearl segment, work 1 sc into each pearl st of previous rnd.

Rnd 7: 1 sc into each st around. Alternate 5 sc in each color, ending with 6 sc pearl. On the 5th st of the last pearl segment, work 2 sc into 1 st.

Rnd 8: Increase in every 5th st around. Alternate 6 sc in each color, ending with 6 sc pearl. On the last pearl segment, work 1 sc into each pearl st of previous rnd.

Rnd 9: 1 sc into each st around. Alternate 6 sc in each color, ending with 7 sc pearl. On the 6th st of the last pearl segment, work 2 sc into 1 st.

Rnd 10: Increase in every 6th st. Alternate 7 sc in each color, ending with 8 sc pearl. On the 7th st of the last pearl segment, work 2 sc into 1 st. End rnd with 1 st st to first st.

Now begin working in joined rounds.

Rnd 11: Work in pearl only, increasing in every 7th st around.

Rnd 12: Work in pearl only, with 1 sc into each st of previous rnd.

Rnd 13: Work in maroon only, increasing in every 8th st around.

Rnd 14: Work in pearl only, with 1 sc into each st of previous round.

Rnd 15: Work in maroon only, increasing in every 9th st around.

Rnd 16: Work in pearl only, with 1 sc into each st of previous round.

Rnd 17: With pearl only, increasing in every 10th st around.

Rnd 18: Alternate 2 sc maroon, 2 sc pearl around, with 1 sc into each st of previous rnd.

Rnd 19: Reverse color sequence: 2 sc pearl, 2 sc maroon around (1 sc into each st of previous rnd).

Rnd 20: With pearl only, increasing in every 11th st around.

Finishing

Weave in all ends. Make a double round of chain stitch edging in maroon and pearl (see Sweet Little Fruits, p. 23). For the hanging loop, ch 15 with maroon and cover with 1 rnd sc.

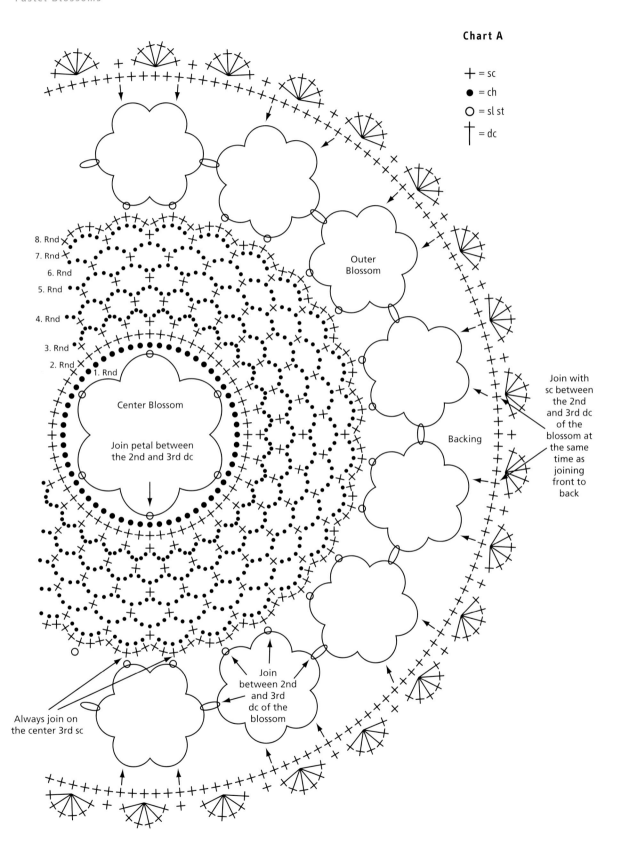

Chart A

+ = sc

● = ch

O = sl st

† = dc

Outer Blossom

Join with sc between the 2nd and 3rd dc of the blossom at the same time as joining front to back

Backing

8. Rnd
7. Rnd
6. Rnd
5. Rnd
4. Rnd
3. Rnd
2. Rnd
1. Rnd

Center Blossom

Join petal between the 2nd and 3rd dc

Join between 2nd and 3rd dc of the blossom

Always join on the center 3rd sc

Pastel Blossoms

Level of Difficulty
Experienced

Measurements
Approx 8 in (20 cm)

Materials
Schachenmayr Catania
in White (color 106), 50
g; Light Blue (color
173), Pink (color 223),
Mimosa (color 100),
and Pool (color 165),
small amounts

Hook: US size C
(2.5 mm)

Gauge
18 sts and 20 rows =
4 x 4 in (10 x 10 cm)

Chart A, p 73
Charts B and C
p 77

Pattern Stitch

Crocheted in the round with sc and ch; begin each rnd with ch 1 and end with 1 sl st.

Instructions

Backing (with white)

Rnds 1-23: Work as for rnds 1-23 of Blossoms and Squares, p. 66.

Rnd 24: Increase in 11th and then in every 23rd st 5 times.

Rnd 25: Increase in every 24th st around.

Rnd 26: Increase in 12th and then in every 25th st 5 times.

Rnd 27: Increase in every 26th st.

Rnd 28: Increase in 13th st and then in every 27th st 5 times.

Rnd 29: Increase in every 28th st.

Center Blossom

Follow Chart B, p. 77.

Rnd 1: Ch 6 and close into ring with sl st.

Rnd 2: 12 sc into ring.

Rnd 3: Sc around, increasing in every other st.

Rnd 4: Sc into every 3rd st around, with ch 5 between each sc around.

Rnd 5: Work 1 sc, 1 hdc, 4 dc, 1 hdc, 1 sc into every ch 5 loop, forming 6 flower petals.

On every flower petal, on the 5th rnd, between the 2nd and 3rd dc, join petal to netting with 1 sl st to a st of the chain loop. To equally space the joins, join 4 times on every 9th st and 2 times on every 10th st, (see Charts A, p. 73 and B, p. 77).

Front

See Chart A, p. 73.

Rnd 1 (with white): Ch 56 and close ring with 1 sl st.

Rnd 2: Work 1 sc into each chain st around and end with 1 sl st.

After completing the center blossom, crochet the netting, continuing from rnd 3.

Rnd 3: 1 sc in every other sc around, with a ch 5 loop between each sc. This begins the chain loop netting.

Rnds 4-7: 1 sc into the 3rd ch of each ch 5 loop of rnd below, with ch 5 between each sc.

Rnd 8: 5 sc into every ch 5 loop around.

Outer Blossoms

See Chart C, p. 77.

Rnd 1: Ch 6 and close into a ring with 1 sl st.

Rnd 2: 12 sc into ring.

Rnd 3: Into every other sc of rnd below, work 1 sc followed by ch 4 around.

Rnd 4: Work 1 sc, 4 dc, 1 sc into each chain loop, forming 6 flower petals around.

While making the first blossom, join the last 2 petals to the netting on the 4th rnd, between the 2nd and 3rd dc of every petal. Always catch the 3rd sc of the chain loop of the netting with 1 sl st. Attach a petal on every 5th sc. Make a total of 14 outer petals. On the remaining outer petals, join the third petal to the adjacent petal and the last petals to the center netting, as described above (see Charts A, p. 73 and C, p. 77). Weave in all tails neatly.

Finishing

Layer pieces and join. With pool, sc around the potholder, joining outer blossoms to netting on, alternately every 7th and 8th sc, between the 2nd and 3rd dc at the edge of each petal. There should be 4 sc between each join (see Chart A). Work the final round with pool: *6 dc into next st, skip 2 sts of previous rnd, 1 sc, skip 2 sts; rep from * around (see Chart A). For hanging loop, ch 12 with pool and cover with sc.

Chart B

Center Blossom

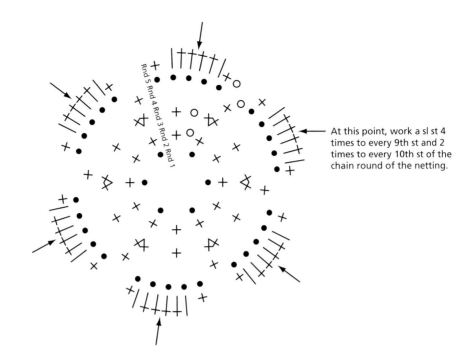

At this point, work a sl st 4 times to every 9th st and 2 times to every 10th st of the chain round of the netting.

Chart C

Outer Blossoms

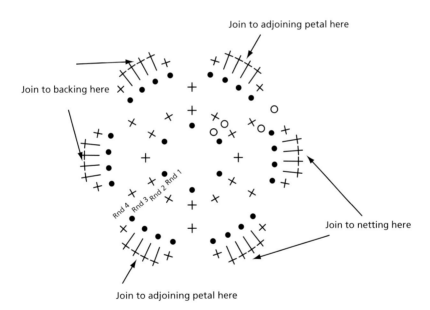

Join to adjoining petal here

Join to backing here

Join to netting here

Join to adjoining petal here

$+$ = sc

$\bullet$ = ch

$\bigcirc$ = sl st

$\times\!\!\!\times$ = 2 sc into 1 st

$|$ = hdc

$\dagger$ = dc

Heart with Rosettes

**Level of Difficulty
Experienced**

Measurements
Approx 8 ¼ x 8 ¼ in
(21 x 21 cm)

Materials
Schachenmayr Catania
in Red (color 115), 100
g and White (color
106), small amounts
Anchor Aida 10 in
white (color 01), small
amount

Hooks: US sizes C (2.5
mm) and 8 (1.5 mm)

Embroidery needle

Gauge
18 sts and 20 rows with
Catania and hook US
size C =
4 x 4 in (10 x 10 cm)

18 sts and 24 rows with
Aida 10 and hook US
size 8 =
4 x 4 in (10 x 10 cm)

Chart
Chart A for heart,
p 80
Charts B and C for
flowers, p 81

Pattern Stitch
Single crochet worked back and forth; turn each row with ch 1.

Heart
With red and hook US size C (2.5 mm), ch 3 turning ch. Work heart in single crochet following chart
A on page 80.

**Make a second heart with red and sc (see Dutch Boys, p. 14) and join the two pieces so that the
potholder will hold its shape.**

Join the potholder with 1 rnd sc in red but be careful not to crowd the stitches or the edges will be
wavy. Finish with a round of "mouse-tooth" edging in white. For the hanging loop, ch 15 with white
between 2 picots on the edging and cover with sc.

Rosettes
With white Anchor Aida and hook US 8 (1.5 mm), make an adjustable ring. The working thread lies
over the loose end which is then pulled through the loop. In this way, the size of the ring can be
adjusted and tightened when the rosette is finished. Now return to working Chart B on page 81.
Turn work with a ch loop and work from the back over the chain rows. The rose petals are worked
from the outside to the inside (see Chart C on page 81). To finish, pull the tails through the center of
the ring, tighten and weave in the ends.

Finishing
Arrange the completed rosettes around the edge of the potholder and sew down along the chain
loops of rnd 2, so that the rose petals stand out from the surface and the threads from the back are
not visible.

Chart A

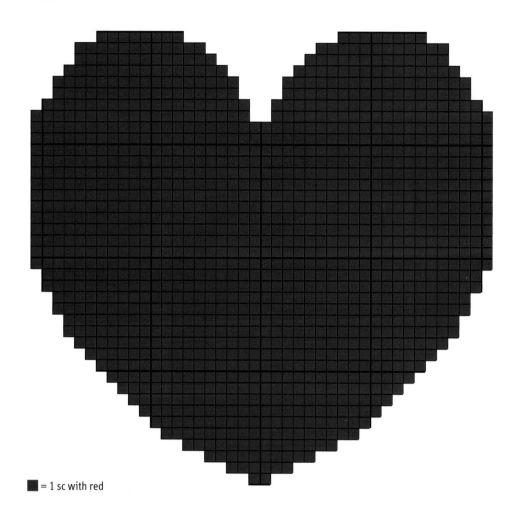

■ = 1 sc with red

Chart B

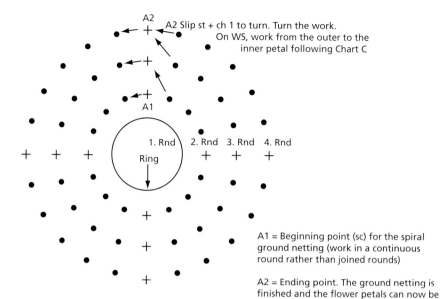

A2

A2 Slip st + ch 1 to turn. Turn the work.
On WS, work from the outer to the
inner petal following Chart C

A1

1. Rnd   2. Rnd   3. Rnd   4. Rnd

Ring

A1 = Beginning point (sc) for the spiral
ground netting (work in a continuous
round rather than joined rounds)

A2 = Ending point. The ground netting is
finished and the flower petals can now be
worked from the back (before work is
turned)

Chart C

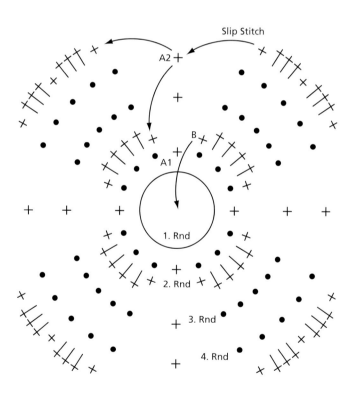

Slip Stitch

A2

B

A1

1. Rnd

2. Rnd

3. Rnd

4. Rnd

+ = sc

● = ch

† = dc

Flower petals

Begin at point A2 and end rnd 4 with 1 sl st to point A2. Next skip over rnd 3 (with
the ch 4 loops) and work into rnd 2 (with the ch 3 loops). Finish at point B, weave
tail into ring.

Blossoms in Diamonds

Level of Difficulty
Intermediate

Measurements
Approx 9 x 9 in
(23 x 23 cm)

Materials
Schachenmayr Catania in White (color 106), 100 g, Burgundy (color 192), Yellow (color 208) and (color 170), small amounts

Hook: US size C (2.5 mm)

Blunt-tipped embroidery needle

Magic Pen

Ruler

Gauge
18 sts and 20 rows = 4 x 4 in (10 x 10 cm)

Pattern Stitch
Single crochet worked back and forth; turn each row with ch 1.

Instructions
Row 1: In white, ch 46 to turn.
Rows 2-51: Work in sc.
Weave in all ends and in spring green, sc once around, then finish with a rnd of "mouse-tooth" edging. For the hanging loop, ch 12 in spring green and sc around. With the magic pen and a ruler, mark the potholder with evenly-spaced diagonal lines and embroider the diamonds with chain stitch in spring green.

Flowers
See Chart
Rnd 1: Make an adjustable ring
Rnd 2: * 1 sc, ch 3, 1 sc, rep from * 4 more times
Rnd 3: In every ch loop * 1 sc, 3 dc, 1 sc, rep from * 4 more times.

Finishing
Weave in ends of each flower. Adjust the size of the center ring and secure the end. Sew flowers onto the potholder.

As an alternative, you could make the rosettes from the "Heart" potholder on p 78 and apply them to this potholder.

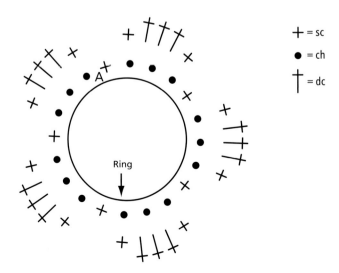

+ = sc
● = ch
† = dc

Rosy Rose

Level of Difficulty
Experienced

Measurements
Approx 8 in (20 cm)

Materials
Schachenmayr Catania in White (color 106), 100 g, Red (color 115), 50 g, and Spring Green (color 170), small amount.

Hook: US size C (2.5 mm)

Gauge
18 sts and 20 rows = 4 x 4 in (10 x 10 cm)

Chart A, p 87
Diagram B, p 88

Pattern Stitch
Dc worked around; begin each rnd with ch 1 and end with 1 sl st.

Instructions
See chart A, p. 87. Begin with white thread.

Rnd 1: Make an adjustable ring, 24 dc in ring.

Rnd 2: Work 1 sc into each dc around.

Rnd 3: *(1 sc, 1 hdc, 1 dc) into 1 st, 3 tr into next st, (1 dc, 1 hdc, 1 sc) into next st, skip 1 st; rep 5 more times around.

Rnd 4: *Working into back of a sc on rnd 2 (the sc beneath a center tr on rnd 3), work 1 sc, ch 6; rep from * around.

Rnd 5: 7 sc into each chain loop around; do not work sc into the sc between chain loops.

Rnd 6: *Working into single crochets on loop, work 1 hdc, 1 dc, 1 tr, 4 tr into one st, 1 tr, 1 dc, 1 hdc; rep from * around, ending with 1 sc into beginning of loop.

Rnd 7: *Working into back of a sc of rnd 5 (beneath a center tr on rnd 6), work 1 sc, ch 8; rep from * around.

Rnd 8: 9 sc into each chain loop around.

Rnd 9: *Working into single crochets on loop, work 1 sc, 1 hdc, 1 dc, 1 tr, 4 tr into next st, 1 tr, 1 dc, 1 hdc, 1 sc; rep from * around.

Rnd 10: *Working into back of a sc on rnd 8 (beneath the center tr on rnd 9), work 1 sc, ch 9; rep from * around.

Rnd 11: 11 sc into each chain loop around.

Rnd 12: *Working into single crochets on loop, work 1 sc, 1 hdc, 2 dc, 1 tr, 4 tr into next st, 1 tr, 2 dc, 1 hdc, 1 sc; rep from * around.

Rnd 13: *Working into back of a sc on rnd 11 (beneath a center tr on rnd 12), work 1 sc, ch 11; rep from * around.

Rnd 14: 13 sc into each chain loop around.

Rnd 15: *Working into single crochets on loop, work 1 sc, 1 hdc, 3 dc, 1 tr, 4 tr into next st, 1 tr, 3 dc, 1 hdc, 1 sc; rep from * around.

Rnd 16: *Working into back of a sc on rnd 14, (beneath center tr on rnd 15), work 1 sc, ch 13; rep from * around.

Rnd 17: 15 sc into each chain loop.

Rnd 18: *Skipping the sc between each loop, work 1 sc, 1 hdc, 2 dc in next st, 2 dc, 1 tr, 3 tr in next st, 1 tr, 2 dc, 2 dc in next st, 1 dc, 1 hdc, 1 sc; rep from * around.

Rnd 19: *Working into back of a sc on rnd 17 (beneath a center tr on rnd 18), work 1 sc, ch 15; rep from * around.

Rnd 20: 17 sc into each chain loop around.

Rnd 21: *Skipping the sc between each loop, work 1 sc, 1 hdc, 1 dc, 2 dc in next st, 2 dc, 1 tr, 3 tr in next st, 1 tr, 2 dc, 2 dc in next st, 2 dc, 1 hdc, 1 sc; rep from * around.

Rnd 22: *Working into back of a sc on rnd 20 (beneath a center tr on rnd 21), work 1 sc, ch 17; rep from * around.

Rnd 23: 19 sc into each chain loop around.

Rnd 24: *Skipping the sc between each loop, work 1 sc, 1 hdc, 1 dc, 2 dc into next st, 3 dc, 1 tr, 3 tr into next st, 1 tr, 3 dc, 2 dc into next st, 2 dc, 1 hdc, 1 sc; rep from * around.

Now, with red, work 1 rnd of sc around each layer of petals, with 2 sc in the center tr of each tr cluster; otherwise there is only 1 sc in each st on the tip of each petal.

Back

Work the back with white and dc only for 10 rounds as follows:

Rnd 1: Make an adjustable ring with 12 dc.

Rnd 2: 2 dc into each st around.

Rnd 3: *1 dc, 2 dc into next st; rep from * around.

Rnd 4: *2 dc, 2 dc into next st; rep from * around.

Rnd 5: *3 dc, 2 dc into next st; rep from * around.

Rnd 6: *4 dc, 2 dc into next st; rep from * around.

Rnd 7: *5 dc, 2 dc into next st; rep from * around.

Rnd 8: *6 dc, 2 dc into next st; rep from * around.

Rnd 9: *7 dc, 2 dc into next st; rep from * around.

Rnd 10: *8 dc, 2 dc into next st; rep from * around.

Rnd 11: Sc, increasing in every 10th st around.

Finishing

With spring green, join the back to the rose layers with sc. The wrong side of the rose petal front faces the right side of the back. On alternate increase points of the last row of the back, join the rose layers to the back with 3 sts at the tip of a petal joined to 3 sc on the back (see Chart B, p. 88). There should always be 19 sc between the points where front and back are joined. To finish, with green, make a round of scallops (see Chart B) around the edge of the back and then make a hanging loop: with spring green, ch 12 and cover chain with sc. If necessary, secure the loops behind each layer of rose petals with sc.

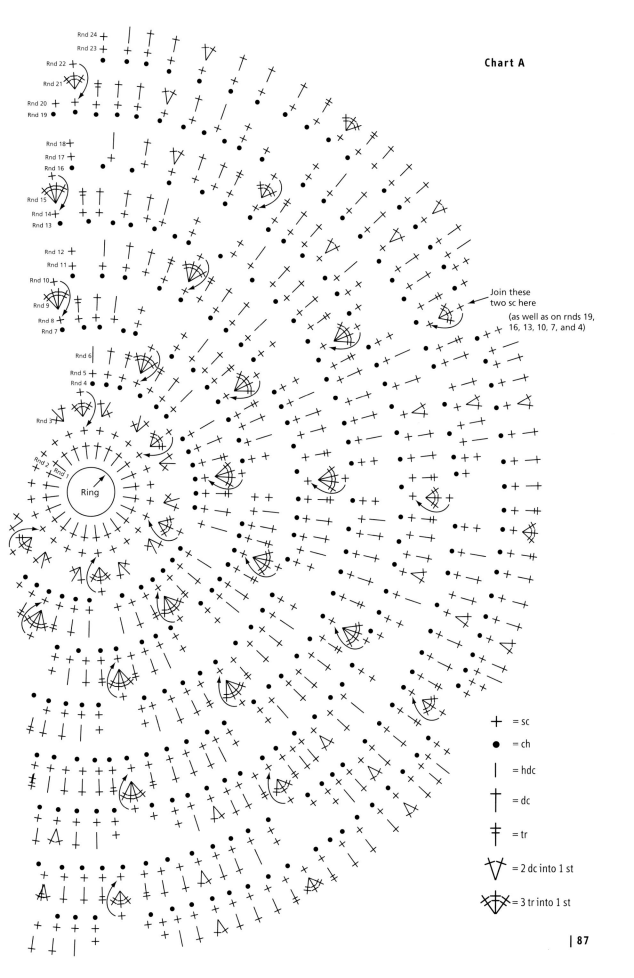

Chart A

Join these
two sc here

(as well as on rnds 19,
16, 13, 10, 7, and 4)

+ = sc

● = ch

| = hdc

† = dc

‡ = tr

⋎ = 2 dc into 1 st

⋇ = 3 tr into 1 st

CONTINUED
Rosy Rose

Diagram B

$+$ = sc – rnd where backing is attached to rose

$+$ = sc – last rnd of backing

$+$ = sc

$\dagger$ = dc

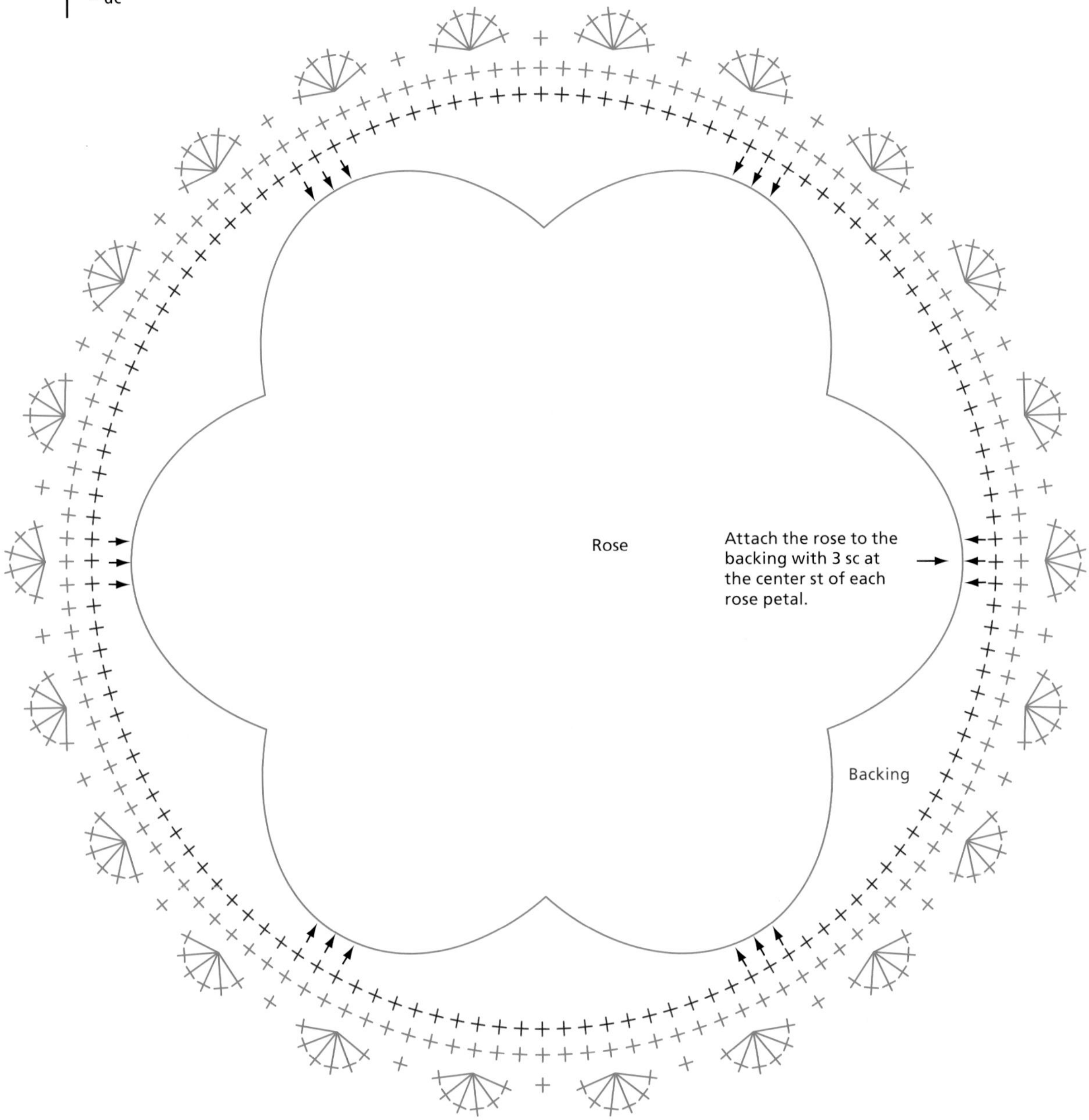

Rose

Attach the rose to the backing with 3 sc at the center st of each rose petal.

Backing

Filigree Openwork

Chart A
Front

+ = sc

● = ch

† = dc

‡ = tr

= 2 tr into 1 st

= 2 dc joined

Filigree Openwork

Level of Difficulty
Experienced

Measurements
Approx 8 in (20 cm)

Materials
Schachenmayr Catania in Navy (color 124), 100 g, Schachenmayr Micro Fino in White (color 01), 50 g

Hook: US size C (2.5 mm)

Gauge
With Schachenmayr Catania, 18 sts and 20 rows = 4 x 4 in (10 x 10 cm)

With Schachenmayr Micro Fino, 28 sts and 40 rows = 4 x 4 in (10 x 10 cm)

Caution:
The Schachenmayr Micro Fino yarn for this potholder contains polyacryl. Only for use as decoration!

Pattern Stitches
Back: Work sc in the rnd, beginning each rnd with ch 1 and ending with 1 sl st.

Front: Worked around with dc, sc, and ch; begin each rnd with ch 1 and end with 1 sl st.

Instructions
Back
Rnds 1-22: Work with Navy; see Spider in the Web, p. 40.

Filet
See chart p. 89.

Rnd 1: With white, make an adjustable ring, 16 sc in ring.

Rnd 2: 1 tr in each sc around, but join the trebles in pairs (work first tr until 2 loops remain, work next treble the same way and finish with yarn through all 3 loops on hook); ch 6 between each pair of tr = 8 pairs of tr.

Rnd 3: Work 7 dc in each chain loop with ch 1 between each group of 7 dc.

Rnd 4: 1 dc in each dc of rnd below with ch 2 between each group of 7 dc.

Rnd 5: 1 dc in each dc of rnd below with ch 5 between each group of 7 dc.

Rnd 6: *1 dc in each of the center 5 dc of group of 7 from rnd below; ch 5, 1 sc in center chain of ch 5 below, ch 5; rep from * around.

Rnd 7: *1 dc in each of the center 3 dc of group of 5 from rnd below; ch 5, 1 sc in center chain of ch 5 below, ch 5, 1 sc in center of ch 5, ch 5; rep from * around.

Rnd 8: *1 dc in the center st of the 3 dc group of rnd below; (ch 5, 1 sc in center chain of ch 5 below) 3 times, ch 5; rep from * around.

Rnd 9: *1 dc in the center ch of ch 5 below, ch 5; rep from * around.

Rnd 10: Work 5 sc into every ch 5 loop of row below.

Rnd 11: Alternate in the sc of rnd 10 (the sc above the first dc of Rnd 9): *1 tr, ch 8, 1 tr into same st as previous tr, ch 2, skip 3 sts, 1 dc into next sc (leaving last step of dc unworked so you can join it to following dc), skip 1 sc, 1 dc into next dc, joining this dc with previous one, ch 2; rep from * around.

Rnd 12: *In the large chain loop (between the trebles), work 5 sc, ch 4, 5 sc; work 2 sc into each of the ch 2 loops of rnd below; rep from * around.

Finishing
Weave in all tails. With Navy, work a round of sc on back, joining back to front on every 9th or 10th st of the last rnd of front. With white, work 1 round of "mouse-tooth" edging. For hanging loop, with white, ch 15 and sc around loop.

Multi-colored Blossoms

Level of Difficulty
Intermediate

Measurements
Approx 8 ½ in (21 cm)

Materials
Schachenmayr Catania
in Red (color 115),
Melon (color 235),
Azure (color 174),
White (color 106),
Orange (color 189),
Spring Green (color
170), and Rose (158),
small amounts

Hook: US size C
(2.5 mm)

Gauge
18 sts and 20 rows =
4 x 4 in (10 x 10 cm)

Chart
p 95

Pattern Stitch

Single crochet in rounds and rows. Begin each round with ch 1 and end with 1 sl st; turn every row with ch 1.

Flowers

For the flower at the center, make an adjustable ring in white. Work rnds 1 and 2 from the right side of the potholder. Starting with the 3rd rnd, turn the work at the end of the rnd and work back.

The white shell at the center is the base that the flower petals are crocheted onto.

Rnd 1 (RS), with white: Make an adjustable ring, 8 sc in ring.
Rnd 2 (RS): *Sc 1, sc 2 into next st; rep from * around = 12 sc.
Rnd 3 (WS): *Sc 1, sc 2 into next st; rep from * around = 18 sc.
Rnd 4 (RS): *Sc 2, sc 2 into next st; rep from * around = 24 sc.
Rnd 5 (WS): *Sc 3, sc 2 into next st; rep from * around = 30 sc.
Rnd 6 (RS): *Sc 4, sc 2 into next st; rep from * around = 36 sc.
Rnd 7 (WS): *Sc 5, sc 2 into next st; rep from * around = 42 sc.

Flower Petals

To change colors for a new petal, bring the old color through loops of stitch below and then bring new color through both loops on hook. The strands will cross at the color change on WS. Work the flower petals back and forth.

Rnd 8 (RS): In every 7 sc of the previous rnd, work 8 sc in one color = increase in the 4th st of each petal. Change color for each petal = 48 sc total and 8 sc for each petal.
Rnd 9 (WS): Work 9 sc for each color petal, increasing in the 6th sc of row below.
Rnd 10 (RS): Work 10 sc for each color petal, increasing in the 7th sc of row below.
Rnd 11 (WS): Work 11 sc for each color petal, increasing in the 8th sc of row below.
Rnd 12 (RS): Work 12 sc for each color petal, increasing in the 9th sc of row below.
Rnd 13 (WS): Work 13 sc for each color petal, increasing in the 10th sc of row below.
Rnd 14 (RS): Work 14 sc for each color petal, increasing in the 11th sc of row below.
Rnd 15 (WS): Work 15 sc for each color petal, increasing in the 12th sc of row below.
Rnd 16 (RS): Work 16 sc for each color petal, increasing in the 13th sc of row below.
Rnd 17 (WS): Work 17 sc for each color petal, increasing in the 11th sc of row below.

Rnd 18 (RS): Work 18 sc for each color petal, increasing in the 11th sc of row below.

Rnd 19 (WS): Work 19 sc for each color petal, increasing in the 11th sc of row below.

Beginning on Rnd 20, work back and forth separately on each petal.

Rnd 20 (RS): Work 20 sc for petal, increasing in the 11th sc of row below.

Rnd 21 (WS): Dec at beginning and end of petal by working dec sc into first two sts; sc across, and then dec over last two sts = 18 sc.

Rnd 22 (RS): Work as for Rnd 21 = 16 sc per petal.

Rnd 23 (WS): As for Rnd 21 = 14 sc per petal.

Rnd 24 (RS): As for Rnd 21 = 12 sc per petal.

Rnd 25: WS): As for Rnd 21 = 10 sc per petal.

Cut yarns and weave in all tails.

Scallops

To make the scallops around the center white circle, work 1 sc in each sc of the last white round. Go into every sc from the upper right, and with the hook behind the st, come out at the upper left, pick up yarn, pull through and work 1 sc. (42 sc total). In the next round, work *1 sc, 2 dc into 1 st, 1 tr, 3 tr into 1 st, 1 tr, 2 dc into 1 st, 1 sc; repeat from * 5 times (see chart page 95). Weave in ends.

Finishing

For each petal, work 1 row sc around edge in the same color as petal. So that the petals won't be wavy or distorted, decrease 1 st 2-3 times at each petal join. For the hanging loop, ch 12 with Azure and cover with sc.

Diagram B

Center piece, scalloped edge

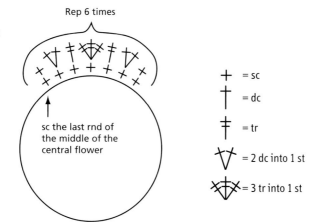

Rep 6 times

sc the last rnd of
the middle of the
central flower

+ = sc

† = dc

‡ = tr

= 2 dc into 1 st

= 3 tr into 1 st

Suppliers

Halcyon Yarn
12 School Street
Bath, ME 04530
800-341-0282
www.halcyonyarn.com
service@halcyonyarn.com

Webs – America's Yarn Store
75 Service Center Road
Northampton, MA 01060
800-367-9327
www.yarn.com
customerservice@yarn.com

Merribee Needlearts and Crafts
12682 Shiloh Church Road
Houston, TX 77066
281-440-6980
www.merribee.com
Merribee@live.com

For help choosing a suitable yarn substitution contact one of the suppliers above. The Schachenmayr Catania is 50 grams for 136 yds and 1245 yds/lb. It is described as a sport or a fingering yarn. Many other yarn suppliers and useful information can be found on the internet.